EMPOWER *Your* SUCCESS

Scott Allan is an international bestselling author of 25+ books published in 7 languages in the area of personal growth and self-development. He is the author of *Fail Big, Undefeated,* and *Do the Hard Things First.*

As a former corporate business trainer in Japan, and Transformational Mindset Strategist, Scott has invested over 10,000 hours of research and instructional coaching into the areas of self-mastery and leadership training.

With an unrelenting passion for teaching, building critical life skills, and inspiring people around the world to take charge of their lives, Scott Allan is committed to a path of constant and never-ending self-improvement.

Many of the success strategies and self-empowerment material that is reinventing lives around the world evolves from Scott Allan's 20 years of practice and teaching critical skills to corporate executives, individuals, and business owners.

You can connect with Scott at:
scottallan@scottallanpublishing.com
Visit author.to/ScottAllanBooks to stay up to date on future book releases.

More Books by Scott Allan

Empower Your Thoughts

Empower Your Fear

Drive Your Destiny

The Discipline of Masters

The Master of Achievement

Undefeated

EMPOWER *Your* SUCCESS

How to Maximize Your **Performance** and Live **Awesome**

SCOTT ALLAN

Published by
Rupa Publications India Pvt. Ltd 2023
7/16, Ansari Road, Daryaganj
New Delhi 110002

Sales Centres:
Prayagraj Bengaluru Chennai
Hyderabad Jaipur Kathmandu
Kolkata Mumbai

Copyright © Scott Allan 2023

The views and opinions expressed in this book are the author's own and the facts are as reported by him which have been verified to the extent possible, and the publishers are not in any way liable for the same.

All rights reserved.
No part of this publication may be reproduced, transmitted, or stored in a retrieval system, in any form or by any means, electronic, mechanical, photocopying, recording or otherwise, without the prior permission of the publisher.

P-ISBN: 978-93-5702-121-0
E-ISBN: 978-93-5702-122-7

First impression 2023

10 9 8 7 6 5 4 3 2 1

Printed in India

This book is sold subject to the condition that it shall not, by way of trade or otherwise, be lent, resold, hired out, or otherwise circulated, without the publisher's prior consent, in any form of binding or cover other than that in which it is published.

CONTENTS

Introduction: Success Strategies for Living a Great Life — 1

1. Create Your Perfect Day — 8
2. Eliminate Your Self-Defeating Excuses — 11
3. Change Your Limiting Beliefs — 14
4. Eliminate Bad Habits — 17
5. Focus on 1% Improvement — 20
6. Direct Your Attention with Deliberate Practice — 23
7. Always Be Prepared — 26
8. Take the 30-Day Challenge — 29
9. Ask for What You Really Want — 32
10. Build Momentum with Small Steps — 35
11. Optimize Your Morning Routine — 39
12. Read 52 Books This Year — 42
13. Push Outside Your Comfort Zone — 46
14. Change the Direction of Your Life — 49

15. Challenge Impossible Ideas — 52
16. Apply the Common Denominator of Success — 54
17. Create Your Environment for Success — 57
18. Concentrate on the Big Picture — 60
19. Shape Your Destiny With One Decision — 62
20. Own Your Mistakes — 65
21. Take a Chance and Risk Rejection — 68
22. Be Proactive During Difficult Times — 71
23. Stimulate Your Motivation — 74
24. Adapt to Change — 77
25. Engage Your Enthusiasm! — 80
26. Invest in Your Personal Growth — 83
27. Prepare for Failure — 86
28. Release Worry with Positive Action — 89
29. Break Free from Perfectionism — 92
30. Control Your Monkey Mind — 95
31. Challenge Your Beliefs About Fear — 99
32. Develop the 'Steve Jobs Attitude' for Success — 102
33. Learn from Your Competition — 104
34. Model the Behavior of Successful People — 107
35. Merge into Your Flow State — 110

36. Be the Best at One Thing — 113
37. Master Your Circumstances — 116
38. Do a Daily Mental Dump — 118
39. Become an Influential Mentor — 121
40. Maintain a Positive Attitude — 124
41. Practice Positive Affirmations — 128
42. Help People Succeed in Life — 131
43. Reflect on Your Day — 133
44. Focus on the Present Moment — 136
45. Say NO to 90% of Everything — 139
46. Plan Your Financial Freedom — 141
47. Live with Purpose and Clarity — 145
48. Become a Successful Minimalist — 148
49. Embrace the Fear of Risk — 151
50. Become an Undefeated Champion — 154
51. Take the Difficult Path — 158
52. Persevere and Go the Extra Mile — 161
53. Visualize Your Future Possibilities — 164
54. Push Hard When You Encounter Resistance — 167
55. Rejection is the Best Learning Experience — 170
56. Crush the Obstacles in Your Way — 173

57. Beat the Procrastination Habit!	176
58. Create a "Things I have accomplished in My Lifetime" List	179
59. Raise Your Personal Standards	182
60. Grow Your Grit	185
Conclusion	189
Live Your Best Life!	189
Reduce Your Worry Habit	192

"Success is not measured by what you accomplish, but by the opposition you have encountered, and the courage with which you have maintained the struggle against overwhelming odds."

—Orison Swett Marden

INTRODUCTION

SUCCESS STRATEGIES FOR LIVING A GREAT LIFE

"No matter what he does, every person on earth plays a central role in the history of the world. And normally he doesn't know it."

—Paulo Coelho

The book you're holding—*Empower Your Success*—is a game-changer in personal development and growth. It is designed to be your mentor and personal guide that takes you by the hand and teaches you specific strategies necessary for building a successful life.

This book is made up a collection of 60 lessons (I call **success strategies) that can be read in 2 minutes or less for quick results. But to make this work, you have to be** *consistent* **and** *intentional* with your actions. Just reading this book will not be enough. You have to read the content, think through the strategy, and take intentional action until it becomes a part of your daily routine.

You must direct your actions with focused intention in order to achieve the results you want.

By applying the success strategies in this book, you will

make significant progress in the areas of mindset, thought, and emotional state of mind. You will no longer have to guess if you are living a successful life, but you can measure this success by the results of taking daily consistent action.

A Blueprint for Empowering Your Success

The ideas that make up this book came about from my 20 years' experience in the field of mindset mastery development. Over the past two decades, I've dedicated my life's passion and pursuit to discover the drive behind what makes people successful…and what causes them to fail miserably.

For many of us, we are "programmed" from an early age to respond to our circumstances. The fears, insecurities, doubts, and all the obstacles standing in your way are blocks within your mind. But once you learn a few simple techniques and restructure your habits and daily routine, all barriers can be removed.

The primary goal of this book is to teach you the best strategies I've discovered to work. Throughout my coaching career and years of commitment to continuous growth and learning, I continue to teach people the strategies that get the best results.

> *"If everyone is moving forward together, then success takes care of itself."*
>
> —Henry Ford

I've seen people transform dreams into reality, and lead lives of incredible leadership, achieve financial success, change jobs, and pursue a path in life once believed to be impossible.

The only difference between the people who succeed and those that fail is this: The achievers believe it is possible. They crush doubt and uncertainty by taking direct action when scared. Successful achievers do it when the world tells them it's impossible.

You can only fail if you fail yourself. By tapping into your hidden abilities and discovering what you are truly capable of, you become unstoppable. This is the path to empowering your life, success, and everything in between.

These "golden opportunities" are available to you, too!

Success has very little to do with getting lucky or being in the right place at the right time. Success is a condition you create by building opportunity through taking the right action.

For example:

- The business entrepreneur who earn 7-figures a year because she wakes up at 4:30 am every morning and works non-stop on her business.
- The comedian who becomes a world-class entertainer because he commits to writing one joke per day (In case you didn't know, this is Jerry Seinfeld's strategy for success).
- A world-class author that, although single and unemployed, spends five years working on a series of books until she becomes one of the biggest names in the world. (Yes, J.K. Rowling, the author of the *Harry Potter* series).

As you work towards fulfilling your potential, remember that everything is possible when you believe it to be true. As you pursue your dream, it is the consistent practice of one strategy that will always work for you.

Stephen King—bestselling author of 65+ best-selling novels and one of the most prolific authors in history—writes an average of ten pages a day, or 2000 words. He has been working this way for the past fifty years.

According to Gary Keller—author of the bestselling book **The One Thing**—when Gary shares this story with people, there is always one person who says to him, "Well, sure, it's easy for Stephen King—he's Stephen King!" To that Gary replies, "I think the question you must ask yourself is this: Does he get to do this because he is Stephen King, or is he Stephen King because he does this?"

That being said, success is not a matter of *who* **you are but** *what* you do. I want you to DO something with the content in this book. That means figuring out what works best for you, and commit to working towards building your ideal lifestyle.

For a deeper dive into this process, you can check out my Lifestyle

Mastery series books right here.

What you will learn in this book

There are 60 strategies in *Empower Your Success*, but you don't need to learn all of them at once. As you read through, pull out the best three and focus on practicing one at a time. You can also stack the strategies and do combinations for faster progress. It's entirely up to you.

Empower Your Success will show you step-by-step how to:

- Handle rejection and overcome your fear
- Live a compassionate life that brings greater joy and fulfillment

- Lead a life with purpose, clarity, and vision
- Reduce your stress and eliminate worry through simple breathing techniques
- Clear your mind of negative thoughts
- Model the strategies of successful people
- Build a greater relationship with yourself and others
- Focus on what matters most and ignore the rest
- Grow your grit and break through adversity
- And a lot more!

How to Use This Book

Empower Your Success is an easy book to read. You can open to any chapter you want and begin reading immediately. You can focus on one strategy a day or just one per week.

The important point is that you practice what you learn. You have to do the work. Not just once but, make it a consistent habit and continue to work and improve the success strategies so you can achieve anything you want.

Imagine where you can be in one year, and drive all your mental and physical energy towards making it happen.

I always think about what Bill Gates said about becoming successful: *"Most people overestimate what they can do in one year, and underestimate what they can do in ten years."*

I have always believed that success is like building a house from the ground up. You start with the foundation, then put up the framework, and finally, design the interior. Everything starts with the foundation. *Empower Your Success* provides you with the foundational strategies to begin building your "dream home".

Empower Your Success: The Series

You can check out the Empower Your Success series for all the available titles. Make your dreams happen by empowering your destiny today!

Now, sit back and enjoy learning from the success strategies in *Empower Your Success*.

By the time you are finished, you will have a wealth of knowledge and be able to practice these strategies to be happier, healthier, and more confident than ever before. I would also encourage you to share this book with your family, friends, and co-workers.

If you are ready…

Let's do this!

"Success means doing the best we can with what we have. Success is the doing, not the getting; in the trying, not the triumph. Success is a personal standard, reaching for the highest that is in us, becoming all that we can be."

—Zig Ziglar

CHAPTER 1

CREATE YOUR PERFECT DAY

*"Life isn't about finding yourself.
Life is about creating yourself."*

—George Bernard Shaw

What would you do today if you could design your perfect day? How would you live each day if you knew it would be your last?

If you could live each day to its fullest free of fear and worry, how would you live?

Many people wake up, get dressed, and simply walk through the motions of breathing, eating, and running to work. If you include three hours of television time after work, your day is finished, and before you know it, you're crawling back into bed and getting up to do it all over again.

By designing your perfect day, you can create the perfect life for yourself. After all, this is what living a life of freedom is about: **Doing the things you love every day.**

Ask yourself:

- What kind of work would I be doing today, if you could do anything?
- Who would I spend time with, and how would we

spend this time together?
- What would I stop doing so I could enjoy more of what I love to do?

Write down all the ideas for crafting your perfect day. You have to feel excited about this! Your perfect day is what gets you up early and makes you super-enthusiastic to be living this one life you have.

Here is an example of what a perfect day could look like:

- Eat a good breakfast at 6am
- Meditation: 20 Min
- Exercise: 30 min
- Reading: 30 min
- Doing the work you love to do: 4-6 hours
- Spending time with friends or family: 1 hour
- Reflection time: 20 min. At the end of the day reflect on what you learned, the impact you made, or one way you made a difference in your life.

Make it fun! Live each day as if it's your last, and live your best life with each day you have.

Here are three activities you can take immediate action on from today.

1. **Create a vision board**. On this board, paste pictures of the places you want to visit and the activities you will do in the coming days and weeks ahead.
2. **Start a goals journal**. Write down your goals. Create a bucket list of the things you want to do and make it a goal to try one thing per week. Will you start a new hobby? Make more friends? Spend the perfect day at the beach?
3. **Visualize your ideal day for tomorrow.** How will you

spend your time? Who will you spend it with? Ask yourself: *If I could do anything and plan my own life instead of having it planned for me, what decisions would I make?*

Action Prompt: Create Your Perfect Day!

Set your timer for ten minutes. Now, **write down what your perfect day looks like**. You won't be able to live this perfect day by doing everything, but decide to try one activity from the list in this chapter. You could start today with:

1. Daily meditation for 20 minutes.
2. Reading for 15 minutes.
3. Writing down your #1 goal for this month.

The next day, do the same activities and add one more to the list. Eventually you will come up with your own activities that work.

CHAPTER 2

ELIMINATE YOUR SELF-DEFEATING EXCUSES

"Keep on going, and the chances are that you will stumble on something, perhaps when you are least expecting it. I never heard of anyone ever stumbling on something sitting down."

—Charles F. Kettering

Excuses live in the comfort zone of your mind, and it is there that all limitations are formed. Listen to your excuses next time you think about taking on a new challenge or opportunity.

Once you buy into an excuse for why you can't do something, it molds into your default way of thinking.

Excuses are misleading.

By believing you can never achieve any of your goals, you formulate the reasoning behind these beliefs. Excuses give us the justification to stop trying. It makes it easier to give up. There is no pressure to succeed, and you don't have to stress about failing since you can't fail at what you never try.

Making excuses is your mind's way of deceiving you. Filled with the sounds of self-pity and limited reasoning, an excuse is very convincing.

Kill your excuses as soon as they appear. Kill them before they kill you. Failing to pursue the things you want in life is a failure in disguise. We use excuses to defend ourselves from the hurts of the world, as we build walls that protect limited interests and fragile egos.

This preserves the limited field of vision through which you see the world. Your excuses for not pursuing your dreams might appear to be valid, but under the surface is a path that leads to inevitable self-defeat.

Your excuses sound like this:

- "I am too old for that."
- "It didn't work for my friends, so why should it work for me?"
- "I'll wait until someone else does it and I know it works."
- "I'm too busy right now. When things calm down, I'll…"
- "I don't have the right skill set."
- "I can't afford to lose that money."
- "It has all been done before, so why bother trying?"

Eliminate your excuses. Recognize the pattern of behavior in you that leans towards failure avoidance and self-sabotaging actions that feed into failing.

Allow yourself to explore the magic inside. Stamp out the voices of your past and feed your mind words that empower you, and train your mind to catch excuses as soon as they appear.

Action Prompt: Remove Your Self-Defeating Excuses!

- Your dreams are too important to be erased by excuses.

Start converting your excuses into positive words of encouragement.
- Make a list of your excuses that stop you from pushing forward. Which of the reasons above are holding you back from doing the work you want to do?
- Follow up with immediate action!

CHAPTER 3

CHANGE YOUR LIMITING BELIEFS

"Put your heart, mind, and soul into even your smallest acts. This is the secret of success."

—Swami Sivananda

The *way* you think has a strong influence on your quality of life. This is especially true when it comes to the power of beliefs. The power of your beliefs determines if you are living a limited lifestyle or a limitless one.

The beliefs you feed your mind are the beliefs you design your life with. If your beliefs are not supporting your dreams or goals, it's time to change the old system and replace it with supportive thoughts that help you to succeed.

Your mindset is not permanent—it can always be changed if you have the courage to change it. And you have the courage to do anything you want!

If you are still holding onto limiting beliefs about yourself that have disempowered you throughout most of your life, you can change them from today.

You should replace limiting beliefs with positive messages about who you really want to become. Here are a few affirmations to get you started:

- I am living a great life.
- I have everything I need to succeed.
- I'm living my dream right now.
- Nothing can stop me from getting what I want.

Beliefs have created the circumstances in your life. When you change your beliefs, you change your perspective of the surrounding circumstances. This is how people experience a transformation.

Remember that you are always in control of your own state of mind. You can challenge the beliefs holding you back.

Here are **six steps** you can take to begin changing your beliefs:

1. Step 1: Identify the belief you want to change.
2. Step 2: Disempower the old belief by injecting doubt and uncertainty.
3. Step 3: Reframe the new belief while discarding the old one.
4. Step 4: Visualize the person you will become once you have created a new belief.
5. Step 5: Reinforce the new belief, taking further repetitive action toward making it real.
6. Step 6: Evaluate your beliefs on a regular basis.

Action Prompt: Change Your Limiting Beliefs!

- It is important to reinforce your new beliefs on a continual basis. Create the beliefs you want to have and do not settle on thoughts that devalue you.
- Analyze where you are at with your beliefs, and whether they are consistent with your desires and purpose.

- Block in ten minutes a day to feed your mind with positive affirmations that shift your limited beliefs.

CHAPTER 4

ELIMINATE BAD HABITS

"It is easier to prevent bad habits than to break them."

—Benjamin Franklin

Your habits can make or break you. More people fail because of their bad habits than from anything else. Sometimes all it takes is breaking one bad habit, and you can change your behavior and way of living for the better.

How can you break the bad habits that are failing you, interrupt the pattern, and turn your fails into wins?

Some of these bad habits might include:

- Watching TV in excess
- Smoking
- Browsing the Internet with your smartphone
- Eating junk food
- Staying up too late
- Not drinking enough water
- Procrastination
- Playing video games for three hours a day
- Impulse shopping

Bad habits are draining, but a system of good habits supported by a disciplined routine can defeat the habits holding you back. Many of us have been living with our old habits for so long that we don't recognize them as the reason behind internal failure.

Break Bad Habits: The 7-Step Approach:

1. Identify the specific problem the bad habit is causing you.
2. Identify the habit you want to stop.
3. Create an action plan for the next 30 days.
4. Review your progress after 30 days.
5. Reset the clock for another 30 days.
6. Be aware of your triggers.
7. Focus on long-term change.

We need long-term focus and consistent concentration over a two- month period to make change happen. If you are expecting to see massive gains after two weeks, you could be setting yourself up to fail. Think long-term habit change and stay focused on daily repetitions.

Your habits are life-changing actions repeated again and again every day. Focus on one habit change at a time.

When you are comfortable that the habit has become a regular part of your thinking, try changing another one.

Action Prompt: Eliminate Bad Habits!

- Make a list of the habits you want to change.
- Next to each habit, write down the reason why you want to change it.
- Create a list of new action steps to change it. Instead of watching TV for 4 hours, what will you do? Instead of

eating junk food every night before bed, what can you eat that is healthy?
- Focus on changing one habit for the next 60 days. After you're confident the habit has taken hold, move onto the next one.

CHAPTER 5

FOCUS ON 1% IMPROVEMENT

*"The way to get started is to
quit talking and begin doing."*

—Walt Disney

The only standard for progress is to be committed to a level of constant and never-ending improvement. You always need to do things slightly different than you did the first time to make gradual but incremental improvements.

By committing to a **1% improvement plan**, you can make gradual changes daily, and if you continue to enhance your performance on a daily basis, within just a few weeks you will show increasing gains.

Think about it this way:

Is it easier to focus on losing 10 kilograms (30 pounds) in two months, or to reduce the amount you eat daily by 20% over the next 60 days?

Could you save $1,000 in the next month, or save 10% of your paycheck for the next two years and achieve your goal of saving $10,000?

Too often we focus on the big outcome—save $10,000 in one year, lose 20 pounds this month, or build a business in the next 30 days. But all of these goals are the result of small habits put into action each day.

Tiny gains that focus on 1% increase in productivity are often overlooked. However, months of refining and making your system better will lead to an exponential increase in quality and performance.

A long-term focus on massive action to get massive results leads to frustration and burn-out.

Here is a list of 6 action steps you can try to make small incremental changes:

1. Declutter your computer desktop by deleting one file a day.
2. With every workout, push yourself slightly more than you did the day before. Do an extra pushup or one more rep.
3. Wake up just five minutes earlier every morning for the next thirty days until you are getting up at 5 AM.
4. Are you writing a book? Write an additional 20 words each day. Work your way up to doing 2,000 words a day if that is your goal.
5. If you're running, try jogging that extra 100 meters with every run.
6. Character is built by deciding to *win* **when the odds are not in your favor. By becoming an** *undefeated* superstar and pushing against impossible odds, you develop a mindset that cannot be broken.

You can save $3000 in one year by making small changes to your spending habits. You can lose 10 pounds in a month by adjusting your daily food intake. You can increase your typing speed by practicing your typing skills for ten minutes a day for the next ninety days.

Action Prompt: Focus on 1% Improvement!

- Identify one area in your life you want to improve, and the daily habit required to achieve this goal.
- Using the steps listed, focus on your one thing and making incremental improvements for the next 30 days.
- Track your progress and manage goals using a productivity app such as Trello, Evernote or todoist.

CHAPTER 6

DIRECT YOUR ATTENTION WITH DELIBERATE PRACTICE

"You can make more friends in two months by becoming interested in other people than you can in two years by trying to get other people interested in you."

—Dale Carnegie

Deliberate practice refers to a special type of training that is purposeful and systematic. While regular practice includes repetition, deliberate practice requires focused attention with the goal of improving performance.

By performing the same action continuously over a long period of time, you maximize the performance by breaking down each stage, one step at a time, and improving on each step. The goal is to make the next repetition better than the last one.

This is the **cornerstone of excellence.**

Focus is the key. You must be focused on the task to do it better than anyone else. Scattered focus leads to distraction and wasted energy.

Focus with intention becomes the yardstick that measures success or failure.

You don't have to wait for that perfect day before you start to act with deliberate practice. You can begin by building intention and purpose into all of your actions.

You must be committed to a system of constant and never-ending improvement. These are the tiny gains that leverage impact on your performance over the next year. Focused attention builds momentum in everything you do when it's done with clarity and purpose.

How can you improve focused attention and continue to build better performance in both your life and at work?

Here are 7 points to get you started on directing your attention with deliberate intention.

1. Declutter your computer desktop by deleting one file a day.
2. Wake up just five minutes earlier until you are getting up at 5 AM.
3. Reach out to one new sales contact every day. If you get rejected, keep reaching out.
4. Create a list of three very important tasks for today. Start working on the first task until finished.
5. Regenerate your energy through thirty minutes of daily exercise.
6. Decide what the #1 project, task, or goal is that you are committed to getting done in the next 30 days. Focus all your energy on completing it.
7. Focused attention brings clarity to your work and purpose. Spend time every morning getting super-clear on the focused target for that day, week, and months ahead.

Action Prompt: Direct Your Attention with Deliberate Practice!

- Stay focused on the task you're working on until it's finished and you can exponentially improve your performance within thirty days.
- Be deliberate in your actions so everything you do drives you closer towards your ideal lifestyle you want. Ignore the distractions that break your attention.

CHAPTER 7

ALWAYS BE PREPARED

"Before anything else, preparation is the key to success."

—Alexander Graham Bell

Imagine this scenario. You arrive at work one morning only to be told that your company is going out of business. You have no job as of today, and this will be your last week as everyone shuts down the office. You realize that you have very little money saved. You don't even have a resume ready to begin your new job search.

If only you had been better prepared…

We know the story well. Life can change in an instant. One day, everything is fine, and the next day, it's all gone.

One of my earlier mentors used to say: "The best time to prepare for a storm is on a sunny day."

Many people wait until the storm is at their doorstep before realizing action must be taken. By then, it's much more difficult to get a handle on things. The COVID-19 pandemic of 2020 showed millions of people—including governments—how unprepared they really are for when disaster strikes.

Your life is full of unexpected events. Money is lost through bad financial deals, family members get sick, or we fail to meet a deadline because of a lack of planning. This is not a question of "if" it happens, but "when." Always assume anything is possible and that life will change in ways you can't imagine.

What you can do today is get ready for unforeseen events coming up. Take a look around and make note of the things you've been procrastinating on. Don't be caught when it's too late.

You can identify the areas in your life that are disorganized and work on making improvements.

Here are 6 ideas to get you started:

1. Save 3 months equivalent of your salary for emergencies.
2. Make sure your house insurance is updated and covers all essentials.
3. Renew your car insurance before it expires.
4. Prepare an emergency medical kit for home.
5. Buy a fire extinguisher.
6. Save all your receipts for end-of-year taxes instead of scrambling at the last minute.

Being prepared means doing everything you can so you can act when unexpected events happen. But you don't know what that could be. When it comes to being prepared for the unexpected, many lessons we learn by failing first.

Action Prompt: Always Be Prepared!

- Think about a time you failed at something because you were not prepared. What happened? What can you do differently next time?

- Take one action today that prepares you for an unexpected moment. What will it be? Be ready for anything even if you don't know what that is. Spend 15 minutes at the end of each week running through your emergency checklist of items that you could prepare ahead of time.
- What are the consequences of not being prepared? Will it cost you money, time, or your freedom? Write down the cost of not being ready and use this as motivation to stay ahead of the curve.

CHAPTER 8

TAKE THE 30-DAY CHALLENGE

*"I owe my success to having listened respectfully
to the very best advice, and then going away
and doing the exact opposite."*

—G. K. Chesterton

Changing old habits and taking on a new challenge is a big commitment. You can become overwhelmed when trying to adjust to new habits, and feel like a failure when it doesn't work. But there is a system you can start right away that gets real results: **The 30-day challenge.**

What is the 30-day challenge?

The 30-day challenge is a set of systematic actions taken daily for the next 30 days. The objective is to achieve the desired result by either doing something new or quitting something old.

You can use the 30-day challenge as a system to improve performance in any area of your life. If you want to improve your basketball skills, shoot 50 hoops a day for the next 30 days. Do you want to stop eating junk food? Replace the junk with fruit…

…for **30 days**.

If you want to build a new habit to make a change in your life, the 30-day challenge is the answer.

How this works is simple: You decide the result you want to achieve and then perform one action each day that moves you towards hitting your goal.

Just think about what you could achieve in 30 days of focused effort. In 30 days, you could:

- Train for your first marathon.
- Lose 10 pounds and cut your fat % by 7%.
- Quit smoking for 30 days…and then forever.
- Save $1000.
- Quit social media for 30 days.
- Read four books.
- Learn 500 words of a new language.

Here is how you set up your 30-day challenge:

1. **Decide your objective:** Learn more? Earn more? Lose weight? Run long distances? Enter a triathlon? Stop a bad habit (smoking, eating too many sweets)? The type of goal you set for yourself determines the actions required to get you to your result. Choose one challenge for the next 30 days.
2. **Determine the one action to take every day.** Once you know the objective, write down a list of action steps to reach your goal. What is achievable? How much time can you commit each day?
3. **Block in your daily challenge time.** If your challenge is to read 5 books in a month, you have to read every day. How much time can you commit to this? 30 minutes? One hour?
4. **Record progress.** Make a record of what you achieved each day. You can do this on a wall calendar or in your notebook.

For every day you take action, put an X on your calendar day. If you miss a day, use an O.

That's it! You can try the same challenge again over the next 30 days or something completely different. If you miss a few days here and there, it doesn't mean you failed. The 30-day challenge is designed to improve your behavior and implement a new habit. This takes perseverance and persistence.

Action Prompt: Take the 30-Day Challenge!

- Decide what your challenge is for the next 30 days. Only focus on this one challenge and don't try to change anything else.
- Record your daily progress on a calendar or in your journal. For every day you take intentional action towards your goal, mark an X on the calendar. If you don't do anything, mark an O.
- At the end of the month, add up all your Xs and Os. You decide what is an acceptable score for success. My success parameter is 24/30 days, or 80%. For the next month I could aim for 27/30.
- Continue to challenge yourself until you hit a perfect score where you achieve your target every day!

CHAPTER 9

ASK FOR WHAT YOU REALLY WANT

"One of life's fundamental truths states, 'Ask and you shall receive.' As kids we get used to asking for things, but somehow, we lose this ability in adulthood. We come up with all sorts of excuses and reasons to avoid any possibility of criticism or rejection."

—Jack Canfield

When was the last time you asked for something you really wanted? Asking for the things we want the most is one of the hardest things to do. The fear of being rejected causes us to hesitate, avoid asking, run scared, and then avoid asking for anything at all.

When you ask for something that you want, your confidence gets a big boost. You realize the fear you have about asking for things is just an illusion keeping you trapped.

When you gather the courage to ask, you remove the fear of asking and eventually get what you desire the most.

How will you know that you can have something if you never ask for it? By asking for what you want, you increase your chances of receiving it by 10x. If you could ask for what you wanted right now, to whom and what would you ask for?

Make a list of all the stuff you have been holding out on. Would you ask for help with a project? Would you approach the bank and apply for a loan so you can start that business? Would you ask for better benefits at work?

There are no limits to what you can achieve if you only ask for it. Even if the response is NO, you still win because you've broken your fear of asking. So, what are you ready to ask for today?

Here are **6 action steps** you can take to ask for what you want:

Step 1: Start thinking about a positive outcome. Push aside any negative possibilities. If you are focused on the outcome not turning out the way you desire, turn it around so that you visualize yourself getting that *YES*.

Step 2: Visualize the action of ASKING, and not the response. It is not important that you receive a *YES*. Of course, that is what you want, but if you bank everything on it and you are told *NO* instead, you'll revert back to thinking about the negative outcome.

Step 3: Ask yourself, "What is the worst that could possibly happen?" You have nothing to lose by asking. If you don't ask, you'll lose anyway.

Step 4: Keep asking. Success is in the numbers—the more you ask, the better you'll get at asking. It is a skill you can master with practice.

Step 5: Know WHAT to ask for. One of the biggest reasons people go without is because they don't know what they want in the first place. You have to be clear about what you want, or you'll end up asking for the wrong things.

Step 6: Ask the right person. Your chances are better when you ask the right person. If the person you're asking has to ask somebody else, go straight to the person who can make that key decision. You should only have to ask once.

Action Prompt: Ask for What You Want!

- Decide on one thing you have always wanted to ask for, but you never have. Write it down.
- Next, write down how you will ask, and;
- Who you have to ask to get this one thing.
- If you don't ask, it's the same as getting a NO. When you don't ask for what you want, somebody else always will.

CHAPTER 10

BUILD MOMENTUM WITH SMALL STEPS

"All successful people have a goal. No one can get anywhere unless he knows where he wants to go and what he wants to be or do."

—Norman Vincent Peale

The Chinese philosopher, Lao Tzu, once said, "The journey of a thousand miles begins with a single step." This ancient philosophy can be used to describe almost everything we set out to succeed at.

From starting a new exercise plan to working on a project, everything gets done by taking it one step at a time. Small actions taken consistently over time builds momentum and, ultimately, you reach the "summit" of your mountain.

Everything can be broken down into simple tasks that eliminate overwhelm.

- You want to lose weight? Stop eating snacks after 6 pm.
- You want to get into shape? Start by doing simple exercises at home.
- You want to save $5000 this year? Start by putting away $5.00 a day.

- You want to write a book? Commit to writing 500 words a day. In thirty days, you have a rough draft written.

The idea is to take consistent small actions as opposed to one massive "I'm going to do it all this week" approach. Habits are formed after months of practice, and even then, you have to continue working at it.

Whatever you want to do this year, it is possible. But avoid the hardline approach that it has to be done perfectly. And all at once.

Perfection is for people who dream about doing things someday but never get around to doing anything because the time is never right. Gradual progress over an extended period of time is far better than massive progress in a short amount of time and burning yourself out.

Taking massive action has its advantages, but it doesn't work for everyone. You have to build up to massive action if you haven't established the proper habits. Build your foundation first and scale up from there.

Every great achievement is the result of taking small incremental steps over days, months, and years. This is what "instant success" really is: Small actions taken over the next 10-20 years.

The best time to start this is today. You don't have to wait for the first of the month or the next lunar eclipse to get going. What is your goal for this year? What do you really want more than anything?

Start with small steps and build big momentum over time. Soon, your consistent actions will reveal what can be accomplished when small steps are taken.

Here are 4 immediate actions to begin building momentum with small steps

1. Write down your goals for the next year. Post your goals where you can see them.
2. Next, take the goal that will have the most significant impact on your life. Is it losing weight? Getting into shape? Saving money for that dream trip or a dream house?
3. Make a list of small steps. These have to be manageable action steps. Do what is possible and don't try to do too much if you experience stress or burnout.
4. Build up your momentum over the weeks and months ahead. In six months from now, when you look back, you'll feel like a mountaineer looking down the mountain you've just ascended…one step at a time.

A successful outcome is not an event but a series of consistent steps. Make it a goal to take one step forward each day.

Action Prompt: Build Momentum with Small Steps!

- Write down a goal you have for the next 6-12 months. Break down this goal into small steps. What is the first immediate step you should take right now?
- What is the next small task you can do? This should be something you can do in five minutes or less.

> "Success is no accident. It is hard work, perseverance, learning, studying, sacrifice and most of all, love of what you are doing or learning to do."
>
> —Pele

CHAPTER 11

OPTIMIZE YOUR MORNING ROUTINE

*"Amateurs sit and wait for inspiration,
the rest of us just get up and go to work."*

—Stephen King

Creating an optimized morning routine can make the difference between success and failure. The morning is prime time for exercise, meditation, self-reflection, and mindset mastery training.

You need to optimize your morning routine in order to live a productive and energetic lifestyle. A successful morning routine requires planning, practice, and consistency to make it a productive habit.

Why is a morning routine important? By starting your day off right, you set your mindset straight from the beginning. By investing in your daily top priorities first, everything after this flows easier.

The ideal morning routine should take you one hour. The question is, what will you do in this hour?

Depending on how long you give to your morning routine, you might do three activities such as meditation, reading, and exercise. Or, you could work on **goal planning, reading positive affirmations, and journaling your thoughts**.

Here is a list of 10 morning routine activities. Some of these will take just a few minutes to complete. You can mix and match these activities, but only one should be your primary activity.

1. Drink a glass of water or a smoothie.
2. Positive Quotes: Read an affirmation or favorite quote for inspiration.
3. Gratitude List: Write down three things you are deeply grateful for.
4. Workout: Do twenty minutes of exercise consisting of stretching, weights, lunges, or squats.
5. Journaling for thirty minutes. (An alternative is writing a book.)
6. Read a life-changing book for twenty minutes.
7. Go over three top tasks for the day. These tasks are focused on achieving high-priority goals.
8. Read your personal mission statement.
9. Meditate and deep-breathe for 10-15 minutes.
10. Eat a good breakfast.

There are three key points you should follow in order to have a productive and fun morning session:

1. Wake up at the same time every morning. This can be at 4 am, 5 am, or 6 am. Most people wake up between 5 am and 6 am. The key is to get to bed early the night before, preferably between 9 pm and 10 pm.
2. Be clear on what you'll be doing when you wake up. You have to have a plan for waking up early. This means knowing what you'll be doing first, second, and third.
3. Optimize your morning prime time with 2-3 primary activities. Use the list above to get started.

Action Prompt: Optimize Your Morning Routine!

- Create a plan for your morning routine for the next week. Evaluate your plan after the week and create your morning routine for the second week. Continue to do this for the first four weeks.
- Then, replace one of the activities with something new. Repeat this pattern and within 60 days, you will experience a renewed sense of self and energized way of living.
- A successful morning routine is a signature of successful entrepreneurs and can serve to bring greater joy, harmony and balance into your life.

CHAPTER 12

READ 52 BOOKS THIS YEAR

"Life takes on meaning when you become motivated, set goals and charge after them in an unstoppable manner."

—Les Brown

If you read on average of one book per week—52 books per year—this is the equivalent of two years' worth of education in a standard university. It's also cheaper to read. With today's technology, we have access to the world's greatest mentors, life coaches, philosophers, and storytellers in our pocket.

Reading a book only costs about $15 if you buy the paperback. It often costs less if you get the eBook version. Nowadays, you can buy, download, or borrow any book you want and learn anything you desire.

This is a "$15 mentor" and provides you with a wealth of information, knowledge, and entertainment. Instead of hiring an expensive coach, you can start by reading as much as possible.

Reading a book expands your mind, opens the imagination, and teaches you anything. Here are ten more reasons to make reading your #1 habit of the day:

1. Teach your family important values and principles

2. Get a better job
3. Build vocabulary
4. Increase brain activity
5. Watch less TV
6. Talk about many more topics
7. Prevent memory loss as you get older
8. Lower blood pressure and heart rate
9. Increase cognitive function
10. Prevent depression and feelings of isolation

Reading is a great way to stimulate your mind. Reading personal development material keeps you motivated while leveling up your skills with new techniques and strategies.

My ten best book recommendations to get you started:

1. *The One Thing* by Gary Keller
2. *Rejection Proof* by Jia Jiang
3. *Awaken the Giant Within* by Tony Robbins
4. *A New Earth: Awakening to Your Life's Purpose* by Eckhart Tolle
5. *Can't Hurt Me* by David Goggins
6. *Undefeated* by Scott Allan
7. *Living Forward: A Proven Plan to Stop Drifting and Get the Life You Want* by Michael Hyatt and Daniel Harkavy
8. *The 7 Habits of Highly Effective People: Powerful Lessons in Personal Change* by Stephen R. Covey
9. *The Power of Positive Thinking: 10 Traits for Maximum Results* by Dr. Norman Vincent Peale
10. *The Success Principles* by Jack Canfield

Reading is an activity that you cannot afford to ignore. I will give you three simple steps I use to read over forty books every year.

1. **Read first thing in the morning.** Wake up, drink a glass of water, and open a book. Bypass your email or even looking at the computer until you have put in thirty minutes of reading time.

    You might have to get up half an hour early to get your reading time in. It is well worth it. This is a positive investment in your personal development.
2. **Choose material that's in line with your goals.** Choose a topic that is in line with your current objectives. For example, I am starting to declutter my house. The book I am focusing on now is *Getting Things Done* by David Allen.
3. **Take Advantage of Small Pockets of Time.** Do you become impatient standing in line at the supermarket? How about waiting for an appointment? I am never bored when I have to wait for someone else. You can carry a Kindle reader with you or put the Kindle app on your phone or tablet. You have an instant library available for reading anytime.

Action Prompt: Read 52 Books a Year

1. Make a list of books you want to read. This can be fiction or nonfiction.
2. Schedule 30 minutes to read every day. This can be morning or night.
3. Keep a list of the books you have read and reward yourself when you reach 50 books.
4. Read with your children, friends, or join a reading club.
5. Keep a journal of lessons learned in the book.

6. Keep a list of books you finish. At the end of the year, share this list with people and encourage them to read the books that inspire you.

CHAPTER 13

PUSH OUTSIDE YOUR COMFORT ZONE

*"All progress takes place
outside the comfort zone."*

—Michael John Bobak

We all live within the walls of comfortability. It is our safety zone where we can control what happens to us. There is little risk in your comfort zone because nothing happens there unless you want it to.

The comfort zone is that space where fear thrives to keep us scared. This goes against what we are taught—which is that to take a risk, to do something out of the ordinary, is pushing out of your zone.

The zone is where you stay if you're completely happy with the way things are. You don't have big ambitions to scale up a million-dollar business or risk everything for success. You could be in a relationship that is boring or even toxic, and even though it hurts to stay, the fear of leaving keeps you trapped.

While your comfort zone provides you with a false sense of security, it sets you up for failure. And while it is failure you're trying to avoid by staying in your comfort zone, you fail in other ways. Your comfort zone is the zone for limitations to stay in control.

By leaving the safety of your comfort zone and jumping into the unknown, you soon find out who you are capable of becoming. Everything you've ever desired is on the outside of the zone, keeping your mind safe from fear.

To take that chance, are you willing to:

- Accept a new job opportunity?
- Leave behind a toxic relationship?
- Start learning a new skill?
- Break a bad habit?
- Learn a new language?

Jumping out of the zone is the best way to set yourself free from fear. You are open to change and accepting the risk that change brings. You recognize by staying stuck, you're saying no to the greater opportunities' life has for you.

For most people, it's the fear of failure and leaving the false security of that comfort zone and stepping into a place of vulnerability. As scary as this is, you will discover the greatest version of who you are meant to be.

Your fears of pushing beyond your limitations are real. The fearful voices in your mind build walls to shield you from taking unnecessary risks. This is why you must ask yourself:

"Am I scared of what will happen if I step out of my comfort zone? Or am I scared of what will happen if I don't?"

Remember this: Everything you have ever wanted to be and achieve is on the other side of your comfort zone. Jump into the Jetstream and see where it takes you.

Action Prompt: Push Outside Your Comfort Zone!

Ask yourself these questions and push back against the fear keeping you stuck:

- What's the worst that can happen if I take a chance? Is this risk acceptable?
- What is the #1 thing I stand to gain? What is the #1 thing I stand to lose?
- What could I lose if I step into the unknown? What do I stand to lose if I don't do this?
- If I knew that I could absolutely not fail at this, what would I do?

CHAPTER 14

CHANGE THE DIRECTION OF YOUR LIFE

"Every great dream begins with a dreamer. Always remember, you have within you the strength, the patience, and the passion to reach for the stars to change the world."

—Harriet Tubman

Have you ever wondered if it's time to change your life's direction? You want to change but starting this process is confusing. With so many options, how do you know where to begin?

Sometimes in life we get fixed in one direction. Thinking that you have to stay the course, you become locked in this direction without changing. This could be a job you're stuck in, a relationship, or your own fixed mindset.

We can move through life this way for years without changing direction, even if the course is taking you the wrong way…and you don't realize it until it's too late!

But here is the reality. You are the captain of your own ship. You're at the helm and you get to decide the direction to steer your fleet. Most people are asleep at the wheel and need a life-changing event to wake them up. You might suddenly lose your job or find yourself filing for divorce. Or both!

But whatever it is that happens, remember this: You can react to the situation, or make a proactive decision. Will you take control of your ship, or leave the direction of your life to chance?

You stay trapped when you tell yourself the lies that aren't true:

- "There is no way out of this."
- "I have no options available."
- "Now isn't a good time to do this. I'll wait to see what happens."

You decide to set your course. Then, you move in that direction and take the necessary steps to move towards your destination. There are **three fears** that hold you back from doing this:

1. **The fear of disappointing someone**. Not everyone will agree with your decision to change course. This could be something that impacts your family or the company you work for. But if you don't act and stay the course to make others happy, you become miserable.
2. **The fear of change**. Shifting your life's direction means rapid change and stepping out of your comfort zone. This can invite fear into your comfort zone. Fear is a motivator to move you in a new direction you've been trying to avoid. Fearing change is only temporary.
3. **The fear of making a mistake**. It's a terrifying situation. You shift the direction of your ship, only to realize you're now heading into a storm. But this doesn't always mean you made a mistake. You can't go back. Only forward. Often, what looks like a mistake in a decision is only the storm we must get through to get to the other side.

Change the course of your life by taking the action you have been afraid to take. You can do this. You're the best judge of your life's direction.

Action Prompt: Change the Direction of Your Life!

- You can never please everyone. Don't just follow a course of action because you're afraid to disappoint other people. If they trust you and are dedicated to helping you succeed, you're with the right people. If not, distance yourself and take charge.
- When you negotiate your happiness to make others happy, you lose your right to control your life's pursuit.
- Take charge of your life by making proactive decisions that lead to positive changes. Make one decision a day and your direction will begin to shift.

CHAPTER 15

CHALLENGE IMPOSSIBLE IDEAS

*"The ability to convert ideas to things
is the secret of outward success."*

—Henry Ward Beecher

To live the life you want, you have to believe in what is possible, even if it doesn't seem realistic. People will always think a unique idea is crazy until that idea becomes a reality.

If you tell people they could double their income in the next year, they will tell you it's impossible.

They could be right—because if you're only making $40,000 a year at one job, and your salary is fixed, you won't be doubling your money if nothing changes.

When you begin thinking about how you can make this happen, you're thinking like a challenger. How can I earn that much money on the side? How hard would I have to work to set up a system that would generate more income? Why do I believe this is impossible?

Life is full of challenges and impossibilities. It is impossible for you to move a heavy object if you just push it with your hands. But give yourself enough leverage, and anything becomes possible. We need this leverage in our lives to move heavy obstacles that are in the way so we can do greater things.

Stay committed to moving beyond your comfort zone. This is where our unique and creative ideas are born.

Everything is impossible until someone finally achieves the impossible. When I started writing books, my goal was to become a bestselling author and have my books translated into several languages while working towards becoming a full-time writer. It seemed like an impossible challenge five years ago. But with hard work and determination, I made it happen.

Through consistent effort, drive, and hard work, yes, you can make the impossible possible. You will inspire others to try and make their impossible dreams happen.

Action Prompt: Challenge Impossible Ideas!

Challenge the impossible dream and make it your reality. Only if you give up and never really try can it fail. If you give up, somebody will eventually accomplish what you think is impossible.

- What ideas have you had that appear to be impossible?
- What could you do right now to start working on this idea?
- Who do you know has made this goal happen?

CHAPTER 16

APPLY THE COMMON DENOMINATOR OF SUCCESS

*"Judge your success by what you had
to give up in order to get it."*

—Dalai Lama

In Albert Gray's dissertation, "The Common Denominator of Success", he researched the common traits that successful people exhibit. These traits are what separate the failures from those who fail and move on to succeed.

In the study, Gray states:

"The common denominator of success—the secret of success of every person who has ever been successful—lies in the fact that he formed the habit of doing things that failures don't like to do."

Take a look around you. Who do you know that is living the life you want? Who are your role models? If the answer is nobody, keep searching for that person.

You must find someone who is performing the habits most people refuse to do. Then, when you find this person, model the behavior and actions they are taking.

What does this person do consistently? Do they talk about their accomplishments or simply keep their head down, focused on working? How does this person speak? Do they use words of empowerment? Has this person failed? How did they handle failing?

Be an observer and a seeker. Look for the successful individual you admire. Copy the actions they take that brings results. Soon, you will experience similar results by building the habits most people refuse to do.

Here are some examples of the habits successful people invest in:

- Allocating two hours a day to write that first novel.
- Waking up at 5 am every morning to work on a future business.
- Setting daily priorities and goals.
- Scheduling reading as a daily success habit.
- Maintaining focus as a key strategy.
- Putting an end to mindless shopping or internet surfing.

The key to personal mastery—and conditioning yourself to fail fast—is to perform tasks that the majority of people won't do.

Successful people are in the habit of doing the things that failures don't want to do. The **Common Denominator of Success** is a model for super-achievers. It is built on the premise that, to succeed, you must be willing to say YES to the hard way.

Action Prompt: Apply the Common Denominator of Success!

- The Common Denominator is about differentiating yourself from the common way of doing things.

- Make new habits that set you apart from the people who make excuses or react to the situation instead of taking a proactive approach.
- You can only live an uncommon lifestyle by acting in a way that 99% of the population isn't doing. This is the difference.

CHAPTER 17

CREATE YOUR ENVIRONMENT FOR SUCCESS

"The first step toward success is taken when you refuse to be a captive of the environment in which you first find yourself."

—Mark Caine

Take a look around you. What do you see? How do you feel about the place you spend the most time in? Who are the people you spend time with each day? What do you spend the majority of your time doing?

For many people, time is served either working for someone or running a business. Some people work from home and might be the only one working, isolated in a single room. Regardless of where you are or who you're with, the environment you spend your time in impacts your efficiency, motivation, and the level of success you'll achieve.

Spend your time with high-level achievers and you have a strong chance of reaching the same level of success. If you're surrounded by people who are time wasters or hang around most days complaining as if the world owes them something, you take on the same attitude…even if that isn't who you are!

The place you work at, the home you live in, and the community you live in, plays a big role in your life. You can't always choose your surroundings, but you are responsible if you decide to stay there.

When the people in your circle do not support your goals and are only tearing you down to their level, you decide if you'll play a role in this or not. If the environment you work in is filled with chaos and distraction, it is having a negative impact on your way of life. It will hold you back and derail your success.

You can only cruise for so long before getting fatigued and burning out from mental exhaustion. Over time, it saps your energy and weakens you to the point of giving up. If you're in a rut, now is the time to get out.

The best environment you can create exists in your own mind. No matter what your external circumstances are, they can influence you but they do not define you. You can choose your attitude and perspective in any situation by building the right space in your own head.

Here are 3 action items you can implement today:

1. **Take a look around at your environment.** The places you are spending time in and the people you're spending time with. On a scale of 1-10, rate the positive influence of your environment. If your rating is below 6, consider making a change.
2. **Be clear about the people and places you live and work with**. Take inventory of your health and well-being. If anything is negatively affecting you, it has to be taken care of. If not, you'll pay the price by failing to achieve your greatest vision.

3. **Manage your mindset.** You control your outlook and attitude towards the world you live in. Take control of this willpower and create what you want.

Action Prompt: Create Your Environment for Success!

- Your environment is either setting you up for success or failure. You decide and make changes based on what you can do today.
- Your environment sets the standard for the level of success you'll aspire to achieve. You need a stream of positive energy to generate forward momentum.
- By setting up your environment for success now, you are laying the foundations for the life you want to be living in the near future.

CHAPTER 18

CONCENTRATE ON THE BIG PICTURE

"Formulate and stamp indelibly on your mind a mental picture of yourself as succeeding. Hold this picture tenaciously. Never permit it to fade. Your mind will seek to develop the picture."

—Norman Vincent Peale

People who are in the habit of succeeding have a clear vision of what they want to achieve. High-level achievers can see everything beyond the obstacles in their way because they visualize what needs to be worked on to make their dreams happen. This drives their perseverance to push past levels of discomfort.

True visionaries can see what lies beyond the struggle. Action follows vision. A vision creates your new reality. You'll always hit your mark when you can see what you're aiming for. With no vision for your future, you have no roadmap to get there.

Start working on your vision right now. Set aside twenty minutes in the morning and evening for this exercise. Sit quietly and imagine the life you are leading.

What work are you doing now? Is this in line with your

goals? Where do you want to be a year from now? Where do you want to be ten years from today? Who are you living this life with?

See yourself doing the work you love and spending time with people you care about. Create your vision with vivid detail. Leave nothing out of your dream no matter how impossible it appears. Everything is impossible until you start believing it.

Make a firm decision about what you want to be, do, and have. By making a commitment, you reduce your fear factor. Resistance is broken by the strength of your mindset. Obstacles are destroyed through your resilience to succeed, no matter the cost.

The more vivid and detailed the images are, and the stronger you believe in yourself to achieve the impossible, the more driven you will be to work for your goals. A clear vision of where you want to be feeds into creating a deeper context for the life you can have.

Action Prompt: Concentrate on the Big Picture!

Big picture focus requires that you take an overview of the complete picture. If this is a project you're working on, look at the project as a whole and then break it down into smaller steps. Every house you see was built from scratch. You have to be big picture-focused but concentrate on every small step to get there.

To create a vision of the big picture, you can:

- Write down all of the steps required to make this a reality.
- Start with one step and work on it until finished.
- Move on to the next step.

CHAPTER 19

SHAPE YOUR DESTINY WITH ONE DECISION

"In a moment of decision, the best thing you can do is the right thing to do, the next best thing is the wrong thing, and the worst thing you can do is nothing."

—Theodore Roosevelt

We make thousands of decisions every week, including what to eat, where to go, what clothes to wear, or who to spend time with. Other critical choices to make might include which university to attend, what courses to take online, when to change jobs or who to marry. These decisions are setting the stage for your journey moving forward.

Now, a real decision isn't just a lofty wish or a dream. If you say, "I want to earn ten thousand dollars per month doing what I love," while that sounds impressive, you need a strategy to achieve this. You also need a powerful WHY for making this your reality.

We all "want" things. We want to be healthier, earn more money, and spend more time with friends and family. But wanting it and deciding you're going to definitely have it are two separate realities.

Everything depends on your ability to decide what you want. It's about developing an **umbrella plan** in which you can envision the plan as a whole. The details come later, but every decision you make has to be followed by immediate action.

You can't get where you want to be if you don't know exactly where that is. It sounds like a simple concept, but many are lost on the journey because they haven't decided where they want to arrive someday.

People fail to decide what they want, then fail to commit to any course of action. And believe me when I say, that "someday" you talk about will be here before you know it. The best time to make a decision that changes your behavior was yesterday. The next best time is today.

Make a firm decision about what you want to accomplish, the values you are choosing to live by, and the principles to guide you to where you need to be. Focus all your attention on achieving whatever would have the greatest impact on what matters most to you.

Here is my simple 6-step process for making decisions and following through specific action to build momentum:

1. **Make your decision.** This is based on your long-term objective. Small decisions made daily contribute to overall success.
2. **Internalize your decision.** Is the best decision now? Is it in line with your long-term plan?
3. **Commit yourself 100%.** Now that you've made your decision, define your plan of action. Decide on one action step each day.
4. **Learn and stay flexible.** Not every decision will lead to a desired outcome. You are allowed to fail. Give yourself permission to make mistakes and try again.

5. **Make decision-making a consistent habit.** Practice leads to progress. Continue to make decisions that shape the force of your life.
6. **Let go of the outcome.** Don't become obsessed about the end result. Take a moment to make the decision that you've been struggling with the most. Then, focus on the actions that will take you straight to your goal.

Action Prompt: Shape Your Destiny with One Decision!

- Today, decide on something that you have been avoiding. This could be a decision that changes the way you eat, think, or how you control your behavior. Your decision might be something you have to discuss first with your partner or children.
- After making this decision—even if it scares you—stick with it and follow through with your first course of action.
- Create a goal for yourself to make one important decision per day, and follow through with the first action step.

CHAPTER 20

OWN YOUR MISTAKES

"Character cannot be developed in ease and quiet. Only through experience of trial and suffering can the soul be strengthened, ambition inspired, and success achieved."

— Helen Keller

Have you ever been in a situation where you were to blame, and the first thing you did was try to find a way out of it? If so, did you claim to know nothing about it, or suggest it could have been someone else?

It's okay to admit this, we have all been there. But the end result is that it does not get to the heart of the issue. This strategy never works. You always know it was your fault even if you don't admit it publicly.

When you make a mistake, it could cost your employer money, disappoint your family, or fail your team at work. We are all human and making mistakes and failing are a part of life. We can't avoid mistakes, but what is important is owning up to the mistake when it happens.

Some people become scared that they'll be punished for making a mistake that caused grief to someone else, whether that is your team at work or your family. When the mind enters the "fight or flight" stage, it looks for a way to avoid the humiliation or embarrassment that claiming the mistake will bring.

There is only one way to really handle it: **Claim your mistake right away.** Make it your own. You have to **own your failure** to come clean.

Here are 5 reasons why you need to own your mistake when it happens:

1. **Removes your feelings of guilt and fear.** When you fail to own up to your mistakes, you're left with heavy feelings of guilt and fear. You worry about someone finding out days or weeks later that it was you.
2. **Owning responsibility empowers your success.** You can make better decisions, feel more confident, and take ownership of your life when you're ready to accept responsibility for your own failures.
3. **Strengthens relationships and builds instant trust.** A mistake that goes unresolved leaves people in doubt, not knowing who to trust. This is true in family and at work. Open and honest communication about everything strengthens relationships. After owning up to something, people will open up and trust you more.
4. **Removes self-justification and entitlement.** If you avoid owning one responsibility, you convince yourself you are right in doing so. You give yourself a false sense of entitlement that says, "I didn't have to claim this mistake because it wasn't my fault to begin with."
5. **Strengthens your character.** Real leaders admit defeat and failure. They own the results of their decisions and let other

people decide if they want to continue trusting this person or not.

To fail big, you have to act big. It takes great courage to own your failures again and again, but it is the best way for personal growth.

Action Prompt: Own Your Mistakes!

- Think about an incident you were involved in where someone got blamed instead of you. How did that make you feel? Do you still think about it? Now, given the same situation today, how would you respond? What action would you take?
- On paper, make a list of reasons to not claim responsibility for your errors. Are these good reasons?
- Next, make a list of reasons why you must take responsibility. Look at the pros and cons of each and you'll see that owning your mistakes and making a commitment to be better at what you do is the best choice to make.

CHAPTER 21

TAKE A CHANCE AND RISK REJECTION

*"Failure will never overtake me if my determination
to succeed is strong enough."*

—Og Mandino

Risk is an opportunity to fail. You avoid putting yourself out there because you've adopted a set of limiting beliefs that are keeping you trapped. Risking anything by taking a chance on a new idea, venture, or relationship feeds into your fear of rejection.

People who are afraid of being rejected, and have instilled that fear as a kind of phobia, are masters of avoiding risky situations.

The fear of taking intentional action leads to inaction. The fear of looking stupid triggers avoidance mechanisms and you go into paralysis mode. You look for a way to escape. The fear of making a bad decision or looking foolish keeps you from doing anything at all.

Here are some examples:

- You don't ask someone out because you think they'll say NO and you'll look like a fool.
- You don't apply for that job you want because you think there will be tons of applicants and you'll look stupid

going up against such tough competition.
- You don't start that book because you think you're a terrible writer.

We waste time and effort avoiding what we are scared of because we don't want to face the humiliation of failing. But, when we don't put ourselves out there, we risk not succeeding, too. We end up stuck in the same spot mentally and emotionally with no forward progress.

When it is rejection you fear, the most direct response to eliminating this fear is doing something. Yes, even when it means there is a 90% chance you'll get turned down or rejected for your efforts. Do it and it will become easier with every rejection.

We can only be confident when we act with confidence, regardless of the outcome. It doesn't matter if you win or lose, you have to play the game. If you don't do something because you're afraid of looking stupid by failing, you fail anyway.

You become fearless by pushing through the fear and doing what scares you. If you're waiting for permission to take intentional action, give yourself permission. Be fearless by looking at your fear through the other end of the scope.

There will always be fear around taking a risk when you step out of your comfort zone. To risk rejection is to beat the fear that surrounds your mind. Take the risk that is just a step past what you are comfortable with. Keep pushing it a little more every day.

Action Prompt: Take a Chance and Risk Rejection!

- Reflect on a time when you did something without worrying about looking foolish (this should not be when you were

not intoxicated). What was the result?
- Make a list of things you avoid because you worry about looking foolish. It could be that you're scared of failing in front of a group, or looking silly just isn't your thing.

CHAPTER 22

BE PROACTIVE DURING DIFFICULT TIMES

"Strong people alone know how to organize their suffering so as to bear only the most necessary pain."

—Emil Dorian

When things are going really well and the world is working the way it should be, we feel energetic, enthusiastic, and active. This is true in our work, family life, and social relationships.

But when things aren't going well…

You transition from taking directional action to becoming passive and just letting life happen. Doubt creeps in and you question if you're making the right decisions. Fear stops you from moving forward and it's an effort to make progress in anything you do.

You shift into reactive mode. This leads to making irrational decisions that rarely work out. When you fail to recover from the situation, you retreat further, leading to anxiety or depression

It's impossible to predict what problems or situations will happen in this life. For example:

- The bank forecloses on your home.
- You wake up and the stock market has crashed.
- A virus sweeps the globe, shutting down the city you live in and your company goes bankrupt.
- You visit the doctor and find out you have cancer.

During difficult times, our first instinct is to pull back, slow down, or stop moving altogether. Frozen with the fear of "what to do next", we do nothing.

But doing nothing is a reactive state. Waiting for a situation to change, go away, or improve by itself isn't always the best approach. There is a time to wait things out, and a time to be proactive.

When you take a proactive mindset and do something to change your situation, you are living your life to its fullest. A person who is proactive takes charge of their life, but a reactive person is always at the mercy of outside forces.

Take control of what you can influence. The opportunity you want is created when you are proactive. Your chances increase when you take intentional action. Your mindset shifts from living in fear to living with a purpose. You become a fulcrum in your own life that can do the heavy lifting.

Action Prompt: Be Proactive During Difficult Times!

During a time of personal crisis, ill-health, or global change, you must ask yourself:

- What can I do to influence positive change?
- What is the one action I could take today that would make this situation better?
- What is the outcome I would like to achieve?

- Get up and move. Exercise or think about your goals. Write down your thoughts. Call someone about that new job opportunity. But do something!

CHAPTER 23

STIMULATE YOUR MOTIVATION

"I spent my young adult years postponing many of the small things that I knew would make me happy...I was fortunate enough to realize that I would never have the time unless I made the time. And then the rest of my life began."

—Chris Peterson

Motivation is the act of doing something driven by a reason or stimulus. There are days when you feel like doing things, and other days you can't get out of bed to do anything.

You might work in a job you hate, but you're motivated to do it because, if not, you don't get paid. You don't want to cut the grass but if it doesn't get done, you end up with a jungle outside your doorstep.

Motivation plays a role in your life at work, home, hobbies, and is usually driven by the promise of a reward. When it comes to work, you could be motivated by more money, a better job position, or the chance to grow your business.

Motivation desires a change and is focused on achieving or getting something. When motivation is activated, we take massive action. When we take massive action, we get a result.

Motivation can be activated in several ways. There are

things we must do no matter what. This is when you feel forced to do it because someone tells you it has to be done. Other reasons are desire, better health benefits, inspiration, to remove stress, or spend time with someone. No matter what it is, motivation is at work in your life.

How can you stimulate your mind to be motivated more often and turn it on when you want to?

Here are 5 areas that motivate you to take action:

1. **Purpose-Driven Goals.** Setting and working towards a purpose-driven goal drives motivation. A goal that is taking you towards a better future stimulates your brain to get up early, stay up late, and work for something you know will bring about positive change. Write down your goals, tack them up, and read these over as many times a day as you need to.
2. **Continuous Self-Improvement.** Working on yourself and making life changes is very motivating. You know the more you change, the greater opportunity you'll create for yourself. People have an innate willingness to change, even if we resist. It's in our nature to want more, desire more, and become better than we were last week.
3. **Healthy relationships motivate you to become the best version of yourself.** Relationships that are not healthy can have the opposite effect and destroy your motivation. This applies to relationships both at home and in your workplace. Spend time with the people who energize your life and encourage you to keep fighting the good fight.
4. **Meditation** is a highly motivating activity because it stimulates your mind and brings peace to your thoughts. Negative thinking will destroy motivation and cause you to have anxiety and depression. Take ten minutes in the

morning to meditate and do this again before bed. Make it a habit by scheduling in meditation time. Your motivation levels will be off the charts when your mind is clear.
5. **Behavior Change.** Motivation can be stimulated by the desire for happiness, feeling good, or overcoming disorders such as anxiety or depression. When you feel bad, you want to move out of that place of pain into a better behavior path that is filled with joy, love, and a sense of accomplishment.

Motivation is stimulated by the actions taken to achieve a specific result. When you are stimulated to take intentional action and work towards a goal, your mind becomes focused on this one thing. You act differently by becoming hyper-focused on your objectives.

Action Prompt: Stimulate Your Motivation!

- What drives you throughout the day to work, communicate, and crush your potential? What do you feel motivated by?
- How will you stimulate motivation when experiencing low points in your mood and energy?
- What steps do you need to take to move closer to your goals?
- What is the #1 challenge you face that can sabotage your motivation? How will you overcome this challenge?

CHAPTER 24

ADAPT TO CHANGE

*"If you don't like something, change it.
If you can't change it, change your attitude."*

—Maya Angelou

Change is a never-ending process that our lives go through. Change is one of the great rules of life that states: The world is in constant state of evolution, and change is happening every moment.

You can adapt to change and grow, or resist it and grow old fast. The choice is yours, but the world is going to change without your permission.

Life-changing events can happen in an instant, or takes many years. Change happens every day either by choice, by chance or by crisis. Change is hard. But if you adapt and persevere through life's changes, you will grow stronger and able to adapt to difficult circumstances.

When you resist change and refuse to accept the situation, you experience a loss of control. You cannot avoid the unexpected events that are happening all around us. But you can manage your reaction to changes.

This is true for people who are used to the same routine

every day. But as prepared as we try to be for change, most people are resistant to change happening. Change is hard. It forces us out of our comfort zone. Life changing events can be stressful because we have little or no control over external events taking place.

The key to surviving change is adapting to present circumstances. You can thrive in bad times as well as good times. Something bad could happen—such as getting fired from your job—and then a month later you find the job of your dreams. Something great could happen to you—such as becoming the CEO of a company—only a month later the business is bankrupt.

Change is neither good or bad, but our perception of how we interpret change makes it so.

Here are 4 strategies for adapting to change:

1. **Confront uncertainty. There is fear in uncertainty.** Change forces us to face our doubt and uncertainty. It tests your level of courage and confidence. When you're challenged to confront the reality of your situation, it's time to face the fear of what you don't know.
2. **Let Go of Past Failure** You've made mistakes and failed in the past based on risks you've taken. Failings are lessons learned. When you welcome a life of change, you accept the risk that goes with it.
3. **Rewire your thinking to love change and the failure it could bring.** Use this as a step towards greater future success. The past is finished. Today is here and your present decisions shape tomorrow. Yesterday's decisions shaped today.

4. **Challenge Your Biggest Fear.** If you want to grow, do the one thing that scares you. This could be learning to swim, public speaking, or quitting your job for something new and challenging. Make a list of the top three things that scare you. Then, identify the #1 fear that—if you acted on it—could change your life.

Action Prompt: Adapt to the World of Change!

- **Change brings opportunity.** We cannot avoid change because it's ongoing. Nothing stays the same. Change can be gradual or happen in an instant. By adapting to the changes happening, we open ourselves to the opportunity to grow from the change life brings.
- **Change brings growth into your life.** By accepting change as the necessary path forward, your mind creates a clear path absent of resistance or fear. When you let things flow naturally, and remember the universe and life is in a constant state of change, everything becomes easier.

CHAPTER 25

ENGAGE YOUR ENTHUSIASM!

"Success is going from failure to failure without losing enthusiasm."

—Winston Churchill

Your enthusiasm is the driving force that pushes you to scale up your life. It can fuel a single idea that transforms your life in ways you'd never dreamed possible. Enthusiasm turns you into a stronger and more confident action-taker and is the juice that ignites your imagination.

Enthusiasm is the foundation of passion. When you feel a genuine love for who you are, you are naturally enthusiastic about living life in such a way that people are drawn to your energy.

Enthusiasm is an action driven by charged emotion. When you are doing something that makes you feel totally alive, enthusiasm is the natural feeling that results from performing the work you love.

Discover what you love to do and push all your free time into making it successful. Is there a business idea you have? A sport you want to pursue? A new career opportunity pulling you to quit your boring job and do something more deserving of your time?

There will be many times when you will lose your enthusiasm for work, play, and the routine of daily living. You will start to question your direction, purpose, and intent.

When your enthusiasm starts to drop, here are **8 simple steps** you can take to ensure you stay on top and keep your positive energy:

1. Start each day with 15 minutes of quiet reflection time.
2. Ask yourself, "What is my main focus point today?"
3. Review your life plan and the milestones towards building that plan.
4. Do what you love to do. When you can't always do that, make it your chief objective to turn your deepest passion into a full-time job.
5. Write down five things you have deep gratitude for every day.
6. Brainstorm the solution to your biggest challenge right now.
7. Identify the one area of your life in which you're procrastinating. Then, write down three action steps you can take to overcome this area of procrastination.
8. Stay healthy. You will always gain the most from your enthusiasm if your health is in top form. Eat right, train and exercise, and avoid habits that suck your energy away.

Action Prompt: Renew Your Enthusiasm!

1. **Spend quality time with passionate and enthusiastic people.** The friends and people we spend time with have a direct influence on our enthusiasm.
2. **Bring your joy forward.** I want you to write down the one thing that makes you feel alive.

3. **Develop an action plan**. What will you do each day to bring you closer to your primary goal or objective?
4. **List the one thing you are most enthusiastic about today.** How will you take action today to turn your enthusiasm into creative energy?

CHAPTER 26

INVEST IN YOUR PERSONAL GROWTH

"Whenever you see a successful person, you only see the public glories, never the private sacrifices to reach them."

—Vaibhav Shah

Personal growth is the foundation of success. It is a commitment to continuously improve your life in the areas of mindset, spirituality, financial, intellectual, emotional, and physical health.

The most important person you can invest in is yourself. In fact, it's recommended by many personal development coaches to spend one hour a day on mindset training. This includes reading, meditating, or one hour of focused thinking such as visualization practice.

Invest the time in getting to know yourself. The investment you put into *you* should be a top priority. Why? You have to take care of yourself so you can be of service and benefit to others.

People who do regular maintenance on themselves are much happier and in a better position to invest more strongly in the world around them. When you're happy and have taken care of your basic needs, it fuels your motivation to invest in all other valuable relationships.

How much quality time do you spend on personal development? What is the one thing you have always wanted to do but haven't gotten around to? How would it make you feel if you could do it? What positive impact would it have on your other relationships?

We have unlimited resources today that you can tap into for personal growth. You don't even have to leave your home thanks to the

thousands of online courses available, which will walk you through any challenge you're facing.

Here are 5 ways to invest in your personal growth today:

1. **Hire a coach or mentor.** This can be a coach for your personal life or a business coach…or both! Working together with a coach can be the difference between success or failure. A great coach can help you work through difficult obstacles that you are blind to. Hire a coach and watch your life and business scale up.
2. **Scale up your skill** through online training courses that are in alignment with your goals. You can get courses on anything today: Confidence building, email marketing, or learning SEO. Ongoing learning creates new opportunity!
3. **Read for one hour a day.** There are tons of books these days to help with your personal growth.
4. **Invest in your health.** Set up a workout routine. You can run, lift weights, do yoga, or cross-fit. To maintain your health now means you could live a quality lifestyle well into retirement years.
5. **Create a life plan.** This is what your coach can help you

with. You need a system of goals to direct you towards your destination.

What should you invest in? This depends on your personal goals. You can focus on spiritual growth, financial investing, developing better job skills, or getting clear on your life's purpose.

Action Prompt: Invest in Your Personal Growth!

- Personal growth is an ongoing investment. For every hour you spend on improving your lifestyle, the return on this investment is 10x. Or 100x.
- You can make exponential growth in your life and the lives of everyone you are in contact with by making personal growth a #1 priority.
- Hire a coach and scale up your life today!

CHAPTER 27

PREPARE FOR FAILURE

"People who succeed have momentum. The more they succeed, the more they want to succeed, and the more they find a way to succeed. Similarly, when someone is failing, the tendency is to get on a downward spiral that can even become a self-fulfilling prophecy."

—Tony Robbins

Everyone who has ever succeeded in business and in life has gone through the experience of failing at everything first. Trying to avoid failure is like jumping into a pool and expecting not to get wet. Not only should you expect to fail, but you should plan for it. This will make the shock factor of failing much less.

Failure is a part of daily living. Regardless of your profession, wealth, or social status, it happens to everyone. Failing is one of the prime necessities for self-development and growth.

To succeed, you must be ready to fail.

The more chances you take to try different things, the more you increase the risk of failing. The only people that never fail are people who never try anything new. They don't accept new challenges and don't have the desire to be challenged in any way.

By choosing not to prepare for failure, you reduce your risk of failing, but you will never break through your limitations. You create a comfort zone that turns into a prison and reduces your chances of achieving any real success.

There is a choice to make. Embrace your failures and look for the chance to turn a loss into a win. You can start today by taking charge and accepting full responsibility for your life. Live the empowered lifestyle you know you want.

The people who fail the most are the ones who plunge forward fearlessly. They are ready to fail fast and hard. Success is only part of the journey, like a goal post they hit on the way, but it is not the destination.

Here are four traits of successful failures:

1. Successful failures embrace risk and welcome it.
2. Successful failures perceive failure as a Lifelong Strategy.
3. Successful failures persevere when things become difficult.
4. Successful failures eliminate excuses.

How do you prepare for failure when what you really want is to avoid failing as much as possible?

Here are four action steps you can implement to prepare you for failure:

1. **Failure is never-ending.** There will always be failures. No matter what you do or how you try to avoid it, failing should be a part of your life. Embrace it and accept it as a necessary path that is helping you get to where you want to be.

2. **Be prepared to change.** Failure teaches us that we need to adopt new techniques, skills, or habits to do things better. If you are failing at the same thing over and over again, chances are a change in your approach is needed.
3. **Talk about your failure.** One mistake people make is, when they fail, they try to cover it up or pretend it didn't happen. They tell everyone that everything is fine and there is nothing to worry about.

    If you ignore failure when it happens, you will make the same mistake again, and you won't learn from it. Talk about your failure to people you trust and get feedback.
4. **Invite the pain of failing into your life.** Don't block it out but allow it to sink into your subconscious. Remember this pain so you can use it as fuel to turn your failure into success.

Action Prompt: Prepare for Failure!

Don't worry if you haven't mastered failure yet. This is a work in progress and you can continue to develop your confidence and prepare for failure by improving your mindset.

- Learn from your failures. You can master your game by improving through failure.
- Surround yourself with people who support your failings and can offer valuable guidance to help you push forward.
- Talk to yourself in a positive way with a voice that is encouraging. Use your positive prompts and read these out loud.

CHAPTER 28

RELEASE WORRY WITH POSITIVE ACTION

"Persistence and resilience only come from having been given the chance to work through difficult problems."

—Gever Tulley

Worry can happen in an instant. You suddenly have no money, you lose your job, or your child fails a test at school. Your mind begins to think of lots of reasons why this could lead to disaster.

When things are not going as planned, your mind flips into worry mode. Worry is always grounded in the fear of the future. We worry when we lack trust that everything will be okay. We start thinking life has failed us, or the worst is yet to come. While most of our worries are fleeting, it is your chronic, repetitive worries you want to zero in on.

How many times a day do worrisome thoughts cross your mind about a lack of money? Does this keep you awake at night? Do you feel short of breath or panicked if you think about how little you have? Does this cause you to react aggressively?

Worry is a form of habitual thinking that sets us up for

failure. You can't be caught up in thoughts of worry and have a peaceful mind at the same time. The way to eliminate the chronic worry habit is to act on the thing that worries you.

Worry is a broken loop of fear-based thoughts. This is a daily struggle with the mind. So, how can you fight back against the loop of fear that worry creates? How do you stop worrying about the future "possibilities" and start living?

Staying engaged in a project or a hobby that you are passionate about keeps negative thinking out of your head. It's difficult to let worry take over your mind when you are working towards something that has meaning to you.

Bringing hope into your life instead of hopelessness in the key to eliminating worry for good. You can build your hope through learning, higher levels of positive thinking, and staying connected to the present now. You need to take positive action and get busy with living.

Taking positive action could be:

- Creating a business plan.
- Working on repairs in your house.
- Helping another person with the solution to their problem.

You'll need to bring yourself back to the present moment, which begins with reframing your situation and life in a positive framework. Are you seeing the world as a scary, frightful place? Are you afraid of waking up and finding yourself homeless one day? Do you think you'll lose your job next week?

Taking positive action is the best way to stay engaged, and when your mind is occupied with a creative activity, negative thinking has less chance of occupying your mental space.

Action Prompt: Release Worry with Positive Action!

- **Financial worries.** Are you afraid of not having money? Get educated on financial planning and set up a savings plan. Create multiple streams of income and save more cash every year. Build up your savings to cover six months of expenses.
- **Kids' future.** Talk with your kids about what they want to do. But remember: You are worrying about something you have no control over. Worrying about the future can become a broken loop in your thought process. It is an endless abyss where anything can happen.
- **Stay centered in the present moment** and worrisome thoughts will not follow you there. Worry lives in the past or future. Decide where you want your mind to be and fix it so it stays there.

CHAPTER 29

BREAK FREE FROM PERFECTIONISM

*"Success consists of getting up just
one more time than you fall."*

—Oliver Goldsmith

The perfectionist believes in a world that must be perfect, and they apply all their energy and resources into creating the perfect environment, the perfect career, or the perfect way of life.

The goal of striving to be perfect in all things is an illusion and the ultimate lie. It does not exist but in the minds of the perfectionistic people that pursue it with relentless obsession.

Perfectionism can be an obsessive disorder sustained by the fear of failure, low self-esteem, and the pursuit of a perfect world that can never measure up to the unrealistic standards it demands.

Perfection is a goal that can never be achieved. You can recover from perfectionistic thinking by slowly changing your thinking. Instead of focusing on perfection in everything you do, focus on progress towards a goal.

It's important to remind yourself that nothing in this world is perfect. A new car still has flaws. A bestselling novel has errors in the story. A beautiful model has imperfect skin underneath makeup.

Things we spend lots of money to buy eventually break, and everything becomes old, weak and dies. But that is the beauty of this life, when we can celebrate our imperfection.

You can only reach your best by allowing yourself to make mistakes and do things imperfectly.

Here are five traits of perfectionists, and how you can manage perfection one day at a time.

1. **A goal, once achieved, is never good enough.** A perfectionist will complete a big goal but not enjoy the satisfaction of finishing. They start to work on the next thing right away.
2. **Unrealistic expectations.** Perfection can never be reached. It's unrealistic to expect a perfect result. Stay focused on progress and making improvements on the way.
3. **All or nothing thinking.** This way of thinking is grounded in "it's either perfect or it's no good." This leaves no space for growth. You can be successful by celebrating your small victories. Reward yourself when you do a good job in school or at work. You don't have to do a perfect job, just do your best.
4. **Critical feedback makes you angry or defensive.** When someone is critical of your work, even if they try to help, you become angry and defensive. Criticism means that you're not good enough, and it challenges your perfection. Constructive criticism is helping you become better at everything. Some people might criticize you or your performance, but focus on the valuable feedback helping you improve.

5. **Procrastination is a bad habit.** The fear of failing is why we procrastinate and put things off until later. The fear of not making everything perfect stops you from doing anything at all. You become stuck, always planning to do something but never doing it. Break down your work into small steps and celebrate when you have a small win.

Action Prompt: Break Free from Perfectionism!

- It takes a long time to recover from perfectionistic thinking. But if you make progress your goal and not perfection, you'll experience less stress and better productivity.
- You have flaws just like everyone else. Let yourself enjoy the process of experimenting, trying, failing, and succeeding.
- Let go of unrealistic expectations that you must be perfect, and embrace each day as a perfect day that you're doing your best to succeed!

CHAPTER 30

CONTROL YOUR MONKEY MIND

"The mind is a monkey, hopping around from thought to thought, image to image. Rarely do more than a few seconds go by in which the mind can remain single-pointed, empty."

—Dani Shapiro

The term "**Monkey Mind**" refers to the state of your mind that is unsettled, restless, or confused. It is the part of your brain that becomes easily distracted, making it difficult to be productive or focus effectively on any one thing.

The Monkey Mind is "chaos of the mind". It creates procrastination, anxiety, anger, sleep loss, negative thinking, and constant distraction. You can compare Monkey Mind to a game of pinball. The ball just bangs around looking for a way out, but never really gets anywhere.

Your mind is a restless machine. It looks to keep busy and, without something to focus on, boredom sets in and the need to alleviate that boredom and restlessness gets stronger.

Learning to direct your actions and not just doing something habitually will put you in greater control of your own life and choices.

You might be having a Monkey Mind moment if you are

experiencing **distraction, loss of time, headaches, or being very unproductive.** The key is to calm your mind through monitoring your thoughts and practicing mindfulness and meditation.

By controlling your Monkey Mind, you can learn to live a normal life without all the constant chaos and disruption. You are in command of your mind and not the other way around. You decide to keep the monkeys locked up, or let them run amok.

Calm your Monkey Mind in 4 simple steps:

1. **Focus on One Task Only.** Your mind can accomplish anything if it focuses on just one task at a time. If you are working on a project that has multiple steps and will take several months to complete, break it down into mini actions. Plan your actions ahead and know what you are working on, then commit to this one action for the allocated time.
2. **Stay in the Moment.** Stress can result from your thoughts when they move out of alignment with your mind. Living in the now is powerful as it keeps the mind centered instead of letting the monkeys run away with it.
3. **Journal Your Thoughts.** When you lose confidence or doubt your ability to succeed, Monkey Mind takes over and pushes your thoughts around. By writing down your thoughts, you can record how you feel in the moment. This reduces your stress and gives you greater control over your thinking.
4. **Focus Your Time in 15-Minute Blocks**. Use a timer and set it for 15 minutes. Decide what you are going to work on

for 15 minutes. Will you meditate? Clean your room? Send an email that you've been putting off? Listen to a piece of classical music? Focus on breathing?

Action Prompt: Control Your Monkey Mind!

- You have to continuously control your mind, or it will control you. Be aware of when your thoughts are running wild and you are distracted.
- Your mind can be calmed by focusing on what you're doing right now.
- Know when your Monkey Mind is active and silence it by talking with someone, journaling your thoughts, and meditation.

"The size of your success is measured by the strength of your desire; the size of your dream; and how you handle disappointment along the way."

—Robert Kiyosaki

CHAPTER 31

CHALLENGE YOUR BELIEFS ABOUT FEAR

"Inaction breeds doubt and fear. Action breeds confidence and courage. If you want to conquer fear, do not sit home and think about it. Go out and get busy."

—Dale Carnegie

Your fears are *self-created fantasies, consisting of the worst-case scenarios imaginable,* believed to be coming true. They are false perceptions of reality that paint a grim picture of how you believe the future is going to turn out.

Believing in your fears gives fearful beliefs power over you.

Fear molds and shapes the course of life in many ways. It is a powerful emotional state of mind. When you are in control of your emotions and mental state, you acquire the personal power to take control of any fear-based thoughts you are having.

The key to having success over fear is *action*. The fear of losing something is a powerful motivator that encourages you to go after it. Fear is a road sign that points you toward the actions you should be taking. If you follow it, you will encounter that fear, and when you do, you realize it was there to prompt you to do something.

Remember that the fear you experience in any situation will never go away. You will never be rid of fear because, when faced with a new problem or challenge, you will always experience fear as part of the natural process.

Learn to accept your fears as necessary for learning valuable life lessons.

Here are 4 simple strategies to help you with managing your fear:

1. **Imagine the best outcome possible.** You have to believe in the life you want to own. When you believe in your fears, you create your fears. From this moment, focus on the best possible outcome for any situation. Imagine the situation you want to create, not the scenario that your fear-based mind is feeding to you.
2. **Challenge the beliefs holding you prisoner.** The most fearful events of all are imagined ones. Take charge and challenge your irrational beliefs and thoughts. Think about what would happen if the worst event imaginable really did occur. It is our fear of having to face the fear that immobilizes us. *What if I fail? What if I can't handle it? What if I can handle it, and then I am given further responsibility?*
3. **You *can* handle it.** Act as if it's already happened. Instead of being afraid of it happening, accept that it will happen and confront it head-on. Fear is what keeps you immobilized; action is what mobilizes you.
4. **Replace the negative with the positive.** Turn a negative thought into a positive one as soon as it occurs. If you think something isn't going to work out, turn that thought around immediately.

Action Prompt: Challenge Your Beliefs About Fear!

- When fear grips your mind, tell yourself: "It is all working out right now, just as it should. I have control over this." Continue this method of fear control until turning over your fearful, negative thoughts becomes a natural habit you can implement at any time.
- Stop believing in fear. Embrace your fear and do what scares you.
- Let go of all thoughts that create fear. Turn fearful thoughts into a positive mantra: "Everything in my life is happening just as it should be, even if it scares me."
- Identify feelings of anxiety and worry. Tell your mind to stop creating fear! You control your mind, your thoughts, and you are responsible for creating your own fear.

CHAPTER 32

DEVELOP THE 'STEVE JOBS ATTITUDE' FOR SUCCESS

"If you are working on something that you really care about, you don't have to be pushed. The vision pulls you."

—Steve Jobs

When legendary innovator, Steve Jobs, approached his engineers with the design for one of his products, he was met with repeated skepticism and told again and again that it couldn't be done. But Jobs had a different approach to everything. He knew that if you could imagine it, it could be done.

Jobs willed his creative imagination into existence because he knew anything he wanted that didn't yet exist could be his if he wanted it enough. Despite the resistance he faced, Steve Jobs became one of the world's greatest innovators. He accepted no excuses, not from himself or from the hundreds of people who worked for him.

I call this the Steve Jobs strategy. Anything is possible, and if you put aside the fear and doubt, you will always push yourself to achieve the impossible at the next level.

It is an amazing thing to conquer one's weaknesses, and

better yet, to watch others around you rise up to reach their greatest potential.

Just as Steve Jobs did, hold yourself to the highest possible standards and do not step down, give in, or give up for any reason. Do not let fear overtake you. Do not live below your potential. Always leap for the next plateau. If you leap with faith, you will make the impossible a reality.

You have the power to choose and be anything you want to be. Dig in. Work hard. Get enthusiastic about living life your way.

Do your work with a passion that sets your life and goals on fire. Seek to inject passion into doing what you love and take affirmative action where you know you can make a difference.

When you fail, don't allow yourself to be defeated. Keep pushing forward until you have built your dreams from a simple idea into your vision of a new reality.

Action Prompt: Develop the Steve Jobs Attitude!

- What is the potential of your talent? What excuses stop you from pursuing your talent and making yourself great?
- What challenges are you going to take from this day forward? Will you hesitate and give up, or will you fight for what you believe in?
- Make a list of the excuses you use to avoid living the life you want. How do these excuses benefit you? What do you have to gain by reasoning with your excuses?
- What are your fears? How can you start to work on overcoming these fears? Write down your top five fears. Now, next to each fear, write down two actions you can take to try to overcome them.

CHAPTER 33

LEARN FROM YOUR COMPETITION

"The successful man is the one who finds out what is the matter with his business before his competitors do."

Roy L. Smith

Engage your learning by competing with others that are far better than you are. Even if you don't come in first place, you know you went up against the best, and this builds strength and discipline into your habits.

In business, sports, retail, music, or science, there is always competition to face. You want to be #1, beat the individuals ahead of you, and figure out what they're doing and try to do it better, faster, and more efficiently.

Many people will copy a competitor's strategy or approach but fail to succeed because copying someone means you'll end up with a lesser result. You have to be innovative, creative, and come up with your own strategy for long-term growth.

You can either keep up with the competition or, lead the way and become the competition everyone else is trying to follow.

Copying your competitor. If you work for a company that makes light switches, you're competing with a dozen other companies in the business. If you copy similar products, slash your prices, and try to undermine the competitors' pricing and marketing strategy, you might get a short-term boost in profit. But copying is for followers that rarely succeed. Innovation is the only solution. This is true in sports and business.

In sports—where competition is a fierce player—you can watch the performance of athletes and how they train. Is there a move that you can implement into your playing style that is different and least expected? Remember that the competition is watching you, too.

The more successful you become, the more people are watching your performance. When talking with people, be careful how much you reveal outside of your professional circle. Someone is looking for that next magic formula they can put into play.

But one more approach is through cooperation. We compete against each other, but in times of crisis when survival matters, humans lean towards cooperation and work together. There is a time to compete and a time to cooperate.

Your competition has several key lessons to teach you. Learn from your competition with these four steps:

1. **Competition is an opportunity for growth.** Look for the strategy your competition is doing well, and try to do it 1% better. Never imitate or copy. Growth and winning comes from being one step ahead.
2. **Listen to feedback from fans and customers.** Good competition gets attention. What are people saying about your competitors? Pay attention to the negative feedback. This is the area you can make improvements.

    A lot of competitors ignore negative feedback and focus only on the positive. But it's the 5% negative reviews that

tells you the skill or systems you can improve for better performance.
3. **Respect your competition.** Good competition is the best. This is true if they are doing better than you. Your competitor is actually a mentor. They learned what works, what customers or fans want, and they worked to deliver. Respect your competitor for the professionalism they bring and you might have a business opportunity to work together.
4. **Learn from competition mistakes.** You can see what your competition is doing right and wrong. Look for their weaknesses and gaps, then fill those gaps by innovating creative ideas that serve customers and create better quality products.

Action Prompt: Learn from your competition!

- Take a look at someone you are in competition with. This could be another company or a friend. Observe what your competition is doing well.
- Figure out your unique angle to implement so that you can improve your own style and performance. This isn't about beating your competition but, learning and growing through watching how they perform.

CHAPTER 34

MODEL THE BEHAVIOR OF SUCCESSFUL PEOPLE

"Success means having the courage, the determination, and the will to become the person you believe you were meant to be."

—George Sheehan

Who do you admire that has achieved the level of success you want? By discovering a role model for success, you can find out what it is they are doing and model their behavior to achieve similar results.

When we adopt the habits, techniques, and specific actions of successful achievers, we can create a similar model for our own success.

Modeling a mentor's behavior is a powerful way to develop personal skills and expand potential. Your model could be a community leader or a personal development coach.

A good model for success is an influential force in this world. They are positive thinkers. The actions and words they live by encourage others to do the same. The strength of these positive words and actions are passed down through generations.

High-level achievers face their fears and overcome problems

and obstacles by working out the best solutions. A good role model shows you that being of service to other people is the highlight for living a successful life.

You can help by providing advice, solutions, or simply listening to problems and hardships. You may not be able to fix their problems, but you can certainly relieve their pain by being there and making yourself available.

Here are four concrete steps you can implement right away in order to *model the behavior of successful people*:

- **Briefly describe all the character traits of your role model.** Write down the reasons why this person is a solid choice for ensuring your success. Why are these character traits important to you?
- **Decide the person you want to become as a model for success.** What kind of person is your ideal model for success? Briefly describe their traits and explain why this person is the best choice.
- **Commit to constant change and growth.** What changes would you have to make to rise to the same level? What new values would you have to integrate? What is the first step you can take to start making these changes today?
- **Be a model for success.** Do you want to become a model for success? What actions would you take to achieve your own goals as a model of success for others?

When you seek out the people who are committed to building the future, you commit yourself to join an alliance of global winners. Think deeply about those you desire to emulate and apply your energy to focus on the person you want to become.

Action Prompt: Model the Behavior of Successful People!

- Your model of success has a story. Find out what that story is and then create your own success story. Even if you're not where you want to be in your life, you can create your story as you want it to be. This is an activity many successful achievers do to set them on the right course.
- Do everything you can to create the changes you have always wanted to integrate into your life.

CHAPTER 35

MERGE INTO YOUR FLOW STATE

"Life is a series of natural and spontaneous changes. Don't resist them—that only creates sorrow. Let reality be reality. Let things flow naturally forward in whatever way they like."

—Lao Tzu

Your **flow state**—also known as being in the zone—is a form of hyper-focus in which a person performing an activity is fully immersed in a feeling of energized focus and enjoyment in the process. This is a state of complete immersion in an activity. It's defined as the mental state of "being completely involved in an activity without breaking concentration for hours."

This state of deep focus can be reached through hyper-focusing your concentration through various means—meditation, work immersion, or time blocking tasks and focusing on nothing but that task for the duration.

Your passion for a particular project or a hobby is the key to concentration. Your level of intensity is dependent on the strength of passion and drive you have for your goal.

You block the world away as you lose yourself in work, play, or a passion project. This flow state strengthens your mental self-discipline, increases satisfaction for work, and gives you a natural state of staying present as you focus on important work. You can get into your flow state by:

- Playing sports (tennis, martial arts, etc.).
- Playing games: chess, Sudoku, or a Rubik's Cube.
- Creative activities: painting, drawing, or writing.
- Working on projects at work or school.

If you can focus your thoughts toward something you are extremely passionate about, you will enter the flow state easier every time.

Here are 5 ways to get into your optimal flow state:

1. **Eliminate multitasking and interruptions.** You need concentration to get into the flow. Multitasking destroys focus. You need to be alert and mentally prepared to get into your flow channel.
2. **Breathe deeply.** Breathing relaxes your nervous system and muscles. If you are feeling nervous anxious, breathing can calm you down.
3. **Perform challenging work.** Your flow state can be easily achieved when a challenging task is met with a perceived high level of skill. This combination is optimal for achieving a state of flow.
4. **Eat well.** A healthy body contributes to your flow state because you feel great. If you're trying to combat illness or a bad stomach from eating the wrong foods, it'll be harder to get into flow. Stick with a healthy diet, eat less, and exercise for 20 minutes a day.
5. **Be patient.** It takes time and concentration to get into your flow state. You should set aside 20-30 minutes to get ready for entering the flow. Use relaxation music to achieve this state, or read positivity quotes and affirmations.

Action Prompt: Get into Your Flow State of Mind!

- Block off 30 minutes a day to practice moving into your flow state. This can be accomplished through a process known as deep thinking meditation, or, Just Sitting There.
- You sit comfortably with no distractions for thirty minutes and focus on your goals, dreams, and positive thoughts. You are in your flow state when the time passes so quickly it almost feels like an instant.

CHAPTER 36

BE THE BEST AT ONE THING

"Success means doing the best we can with what we have. Success is the doing, not the getting; in the trying, not the triumph. Success is a personal standard, reaching for the highest that is in us, becoming all that we can be."

—Zig Ziglar

It's estimated that it takes about 10,000 hours of practice time to master one specific skill. That is only if you can commit to working on this skill for 4 hours a day for the next five years.

Today, we have unlimited applications and technology marketed to help us master anything in just days, weeks, or months. But technology can't replace the common practice of hard work. Most people aren't that patient. They work on something for a few weeks or months, and after making some improvement, move onto something else.

If this is your plan, you will become average at a lot of things but master nothing. Would you rather be good at ten things, or the master of just one?

Being average isn't the same as developing mastery. To be the best at one thing takes commitment. You must be intentional in scheduling your time to work on your skill. This is true if you play guitar, paint a picture, write a book, or learn to negotiate in business for your company.

You must commit to the practice of constant learning, doing, failing, and continue to improve every day. People who master a skill are focusing on only this one skill. Everything else is a distraction. The key to this approach is to block out your distractions and stay committed to your course of action leading to the outcome you really want.

You can only be the best at one thing when you know what that is. If you're uncertain about what that is, then everything becomes a shiny object you continuously chase without any results.

It takes about 66 days to fully implement a new habit into your lifestyle. But after this becomes a habit, you have to continue practicing. You need a plan for when you will do this, how you'll do it, and what it is you're doing.

When? Is it at 9 am every morning for 2 hours?

How? What is the action step you're taking? What activity are you implementing?

What? What is the skill you're mastering? You should write this down so you can stay on course.

Anyone can master their passion if they truly love what they are doing. But you have to want to master your one thing and stick with a plan to work hard at it. There are no easy shortcuts.

Here is a **4-step simple plan** to become the master of your one thing:

1. **Commit to daily practice**. Make a commitment with yourself to practice every day. It's okay to take a day off per week, but don't let this be a long gap in your training.

2. **Time block training time**. Block in 2 hours a day to practice the skill you wish to master.
3. **Focus on one thing only.** If you are trying to master 2-5 skills, you will be average at all of them.
4. **Keep practicing.** When you are tired, work at it. When you want to give up, work at it.

Action Prompt: Be the Best at One Thing!

- You have to train consistently. Learn from the mistakes you make. Stick with it even on the days you don't want to. This is when you must practice the hardest. You can only master something when you show up every day to work at it.
- Commit to mastery of that one skill and you will hone in on your one passion that can change everything. Master of one is master of all.
- Ignore your distractions to start something new when focusing on your one thing to master.

CHAPTER 37

MASTER YOUR CIRCUMSTANCES

*"The first step toward success is taken
when you refuse to be a captive of the
environment in which you first find yourself."*

—Mark Caine

If you can't discipline yourself to master your surrounding circumstances, you will end up becoming controlled by them. The circumstances we are referring to are those situations in life that are not created by you but govern your right to freedom.

A life by design and not by default is about taking intentional actions to change, shape, and develop your future instead of allowing it to happen by luck or chance.

You're never a victim of your circumstances. You are the master of your circumstances. While you may not be able to control what happens, you can decide how you deal with it.

What will you do if…

- your business crashes and you have to start over?
- your spouse decides to divorce you?
- you lose your job because of layoffs?
- you're in an accident and permanently injured?

We don't know what challenges life will bring. One day, things are fine, and the next, you might be locked in a struggle to survive.

What we do know is that you can be the master of your actions. You can master your emotions, and thus, master the decisions that influence your destiny. This is how you live by design and not by default.

When we rely on default to work things out, it is throwing chance to the wind and hoping for the best. In this case, you have no control over the outcome and are relying on blind luck to get through.

You're either living an empowered lifestyle governed by intentional action, or you exist to serve someone else's agenda.

By design, you are the master of your life. By default, you become a slave to somebody else's plan.

We can always maximize our quality of life by staying fixed on the things that matter most and avoiding whatever doesn't add value.

Action Prompt: Master Your Circumstances!

- **Throw away your "life by default" attitude.** Throw away the attitude that says it will all work out even if you do nothing. You can pray for the best, but as soon as you are done, get to work on building the best. Success is not an accident but a planned event.
- **Be aware of the obstacles keeping you stuck.** Make a list of the challenges you have every day, even if it is something as simple as making a call or filling out a form. If something is blocking you, work to remove it and keep chipping away until it is done.

CHAPTER 38

DO A DAILY MENTAL DUMP

*"Excellence is an art won by
training and habituation."*

—Aristotle

Can you imagine if, instead of taking your garbage out every week, you let it pile up in your kitchen for a few months? This is hard to imagine. But, if you think about it, that is what we do with our worries, thoughts, and negative emotions.

We hold on to old memories, rethink the same problems over and over, and feed into negative thoughts even when they make us miserable.

In a single day, we can have from 50,000 to 70,000 thoughts. At the end of the day, we are exhausted, but it isn't just from working all day. Our build-up of thoughts puts a heavy burden on the brain and can create overload, draining us of mental energy.

You need to decompress your thoughts throughout the day. Starting things right and finishing off with a mental dump of your ideas. This "mental dump" will make sure you can refresh your mind for the next day. Why hold onto old thoughts and worries from yesterday, last week, or last year? What you need is a mental dump of all your thoughts at the end of the day.

I recommend ten minutes of focused thinking every evening before bed. Instead of watching TV or surfing Social Share sites, you are going to set up a ten-minute 'mental dump' block to remove the garbage that has accumulated in your mind.

If you do this at the end of each day, you can wake up refreshed. Your mental energy will be restored and you can start with a full tank of enthusiasm instead of a mind running on empty.

Don't wait until something is broken before fixing it. Schedule time throughout the day to decompress. You don't have to wait until your mind is overflowing with stress, worry, and negative thinking before you take action.

This 5-step process is your daily habit for cleaning your 'mental house' at the end of each day.

1. **Create a gratitude list.** Make a list of five people you are grateful for in your life. Next to each name, state in one sentence why you are grateful for this person in your life.
2. **Let go of resentment**. Think about the one person you are harboring resentment against. Release your negative thoughts about this person by sending out positive words of encouragement.
3. **Express your gratitude** to the people in your life that they are here with you for another day.
4. **Burn negative thoughts**. Imagine taking all your thoughts and throwing them into a big fire. Watch them burn in your mind. This improves the quality of your sleep and you're free to start fresh the next day.
5. **Writing down your thoughts will empty your mind of old ideas.** Your negative thoughts can pile up and damage your mindset over time. Writing down your thoughts as

they occur forces your mind to generate new ideas that have been buried under old thinking.

Action Prompt: Do a daily mental dump!

- Schedule 10-15 minutes as part of your routine to wind down. Turn off all of your devices. Using the 5-step process, in your journal write down your thoughts and dump everything on paper.
- Make a list of people you helped and people you harmed. Get clear on your actions that you took during the day.
- Ask yourself: What will I do differently tomorrow? Who will I connect with? What is the one thing I can improve on?

CHAPTER 39

BECOME AN INFLUENTIAL MENTOR

*"There are two types of people who will
tell you that you cannot make a difference
in this world: those who are afraid to try
and those who are afraid you will succeed."*

—Ray Goforth

There are mentors for every area of life. You could be the person who helps someone overcome their challenges and succeed. If you are ready to **make a difference** and help people transform their lives, it is time to become a mentor.

Mentoring plays a dominant role in the development of our people and the world in which we live. The mentoring relationship is an opportunity to take on a new role in life. It is a chance to participate in the growth and development of another person through working together to build a positive relationship.

You are providing a valuable service to people so they can benefit and grow from your experiences and wisdom.

Mentoring is a unique blend of a deep, personal friendship, mutual growth, and an open and honest channel of communication with another human being.

A good mentor helps another person learn to tap into their true potential for achieving higher levels of success. From business to family, and in relationships that evolve to form a solid partnership, a spiritual transition occurs.

You do not need special training to become a mentor; believing otherwise is a common misconception. All you need is a burning desire

to help others. The only training, special skills, or knowledge required is what you already have with you, which is a lifetime of experience

Look for the opportunity to share your message and make a difference in someone else's life. One simple act of kindness, a hand that reaches down and helps another person up, will be remembered.

Here are 7 steps to become a mentor for someone today:

1. Helps to clarify and determine goals, and to build a vision that supports the success of those goals
2. Helps to identify self-destructive habits and negative beliefs by offering suggestions or a course of action to take the mentee to a place of personal empowerment
3. Nurturing unique talents and interests so they can merge with their chosen path and fulfill their role in this world
4. Listens with genuine interest to the partner and guides them to discover solutions to problems through asking pertinent questions related to their area of concern
5. Encourages people to expand their horizons—that is, to stretch out into the world, pushing beyond their comfort zone so they are more comfortable with taking risks and trying new things

6. Assists the mentee to build strong character values in line with the person they most desire to become
7. Shares their own unique experiences with the mentee, offering helpful insights while demonstrating a genuine enthusiasm and willingness to be there when needed

Action Prompt: Become an Influential Mentor!

- As mentors, we must strive to attain certain vital characteristics if we are to become effective leaders. This requires a passion for service in helping others to grow and succeed. It needs an investment of your time, as well as a solid commitment to the individual. Take a look around you. Who can you mentor? Who needs your help?

CHAPTER 40

MAINTAIN A POSITIVE ATTITUDE

"Whenever you're in conflict with someone, there is one factor that can make the difference between damaging your relationship and deepening it. That factor is attitude."

—William James

Your positive mental attitude is the pillar of success in everything you do. Your positive attitude is a projection of your thoughts, values, and feelings stretching out into the world.

When you hold in negative emotions, it defines your entire attitude. Your actions, words, and facial expressions tell people what you're feeling, thinking, and experiencing.

Attitude is always transparent. You can feel it when communicating with someone. A positive attitude makes other people feel good. You can raise the energy of the people around you by expressing positive emotions that result from your positive attitude.

Your positive mindset is critical for 8 reasons because you:

1. Attract the right people and circumstances to help you succeed.

2. Maintain a peaceful mind that uses mindfulness to stay focused on the present moment.
3. Become financially affluent.
4. Remove self-imposed limitations.
5. Experience less stress and more control over your reactions.
6. See anything as possible, so you are less scared to try new challenges.
7. Gain a positive outlook on the future.
8. Laugh more, exercise regularly, eat better, and live longer.

A positive mental attitude creates positive energy. It has a profound impact on your perspective. Developing a positive mindset sets you up for all your future wins. It is the key to attracting opportunities and building the life you want.

In directing your positive attitude by choice, you will be in control of the way you view the world. Having a positive mindset creates better success in your work, family, and relationships.

Focusing on positive thoughts and following through with equally powerful actions creates a new attitude shift. Focusing on building a positive mindset is the first thing you should do. It is the rock-solid foundation for creating a quality lifestyle.

Action Prompt: Maintain a Positive Attitude!

- Close the door on your past failures.
- Clear your mind every morning and evening of negative influence that doesn't contribute towards your positive mindset
- Focus on learning a new skill or sharpening your mindset

so you don't fall back into lazy thinking.
- Be the boss of your own mind. You control everything that is being created in your head. Own it.

"The key to success is action, and the essential in action is perseverance."

—Sun Yat-sen

CHAPTER 41

PRACTICE POSITIVE AFFIRMATIONS

> *"I begin each day with prayer and meditation.
> Throughout the day, I use affirmations and
> positive intentions to move through blocks, and
> each evening, I close the day with self-reflection and
> an inventory of my growth throughout the day."*
>
> —Gabrielle Bernstein

A positive affirmation is a form of internal reprogramming designed to replace the internal recordings you have been listening to unconsciously for most of your life. Affirmations help you to rewire your brain by focusing on what your heart desires the most.

An affirmation, or mantra, is a powerful method of convincing the subconscious mind that a belief or situation already exists. Affirmations are detailed statements of you living and enjoying life as if everything you've ever wanted has already been achieved or is becoming your reality in this moment.

Some examples of affirmations are:

"I can handle any difficult situation with serenity and confidence, seeking the best solution that is fair and just."

"My life is in the right place and I am where I need to be to

learn, grow, and make the progress necessary for the advancement of my destiny."

"There isn't any difficulty or situation that I cannot handle, no problem is too big, and as long as I stay positive and in the now, I trust I will do the right thing."

"I have all that I need to be happy and I am completely satisfied."

"I am an honest, confident, capable person with compassion for all things."

"I am the master of my destiny, the creator of my world."

"All difficult people and situations are there to make me a stronger and better person."

Through consistently creating and repeating positive statements to yourself, you can turn off the inner rampant dialogue that has been running things and replace it with healthier, more vibrant words of choice that express the emotions and experiences you desire to create.

Here are the **5 guidelines** when creating your own affirmations:

1. An affirmation is always positive and said in the present tense.
2. Affirmations are short, concise, and to the point.
3. An affirmation is personal. It focuses on a belief, value, or principle you desire to integrate into your mental functions.
4. An affirmation conveys emotion and feelings.
5. Affirmations support your deepest values and always express the person you are striving to become.

Action Prompt: Practice Positive Affirmations!

- Create some of your own affirmations to use every day and enjoy the state of relaxation they bring you. You can also create affirmations for your goals and act as if your goals have been achieved already!
- Begin to compile a list of affirmations by writing down positive statements about yourself, your life, and about other people. Add one new affirmation to this list every day.

CHAPTER 42

HELP PEOPLE SUCCEED IN LIFE

*"I believe that the most meaningful way
to succeed is to help other people succeed."*

—Adam Grant

Every day is an opportunity to be of service to other people. We are often so preoccupied with our own worries, fears, and needs that we fail to see the struggles people around us are carrying. To add to this confusion, we now have smartphones, devices, games, and computers that pull our attention away from helping other people.

People have become too focused on one thing…themselves! This unhealthy focus needs to be reverted in order for you to be that helping hand for someone who needs it.

Helping a fellow human being not only helps the other person but that person will feel so grateful, they will do the same things for someone else. Helping people makes you feel great about yourself, improves the lives of others, and adds kindness to a world that needs more of it.

One simple act of kindness has a long-lasting impact. It moves from person to person. Make people smile and give them hope that there are kind people who do care.

Here are 6 simple steps you can practice to start helping people today:

1. **Stop to help.** Last week, I watched a woman help another woman pick up her bicycle after it had fallen over.
2. **Give away your stuff.** Do you have clothes, furniture, or office supplies no longer in use? Find someone that needs them before throwing it away.
3. **Listen to someone.** If someone is having a bad day or going through a difficult time, they might need to talk with someone who can listen.
4. **Send a birthday card.** Know someone with a birthday coming up? Send that person a card, either an e-card or mail the real thing.
5. **Send a nice email**. Just a quick note telling someone how much you appreciate them, how proud you are of them, or saying thank you for something they did well.
6. **Give praise for a good job.** If someone does a good job, the best thing you can do is show how much you appreciate them. Give kind words to compliment them when they are trying hard to be good at their work. You can do this at work or at home with your family.

Action Prompt: Help People!

- Look for every chance to help people when they need it. People don't always ask for help, so you have to look for the opportunity to reach out and offer to help them. This could be an unforgettable act that they will always remember.
- Set a goal to help one person every day. This can be anything, but you must commit to this goal for 30 days. Just imagine how many people you could help in just 30 days!

CHAPTER 43

REFLECT ON YOUR DAY

"I feel really grateful to the people who encouraged me and helped me develop. Nobody can succeed on their own."

—Sheryl Sandberg

My favorite habit at the end of the day is to sit quietly for fifteen minutes and reflect on everything that happened during the day. Who did I talk to? What did I work on? What did I learn today? What technique or skill did I improve? What mistakes did I learn from? Was I successful in living this day the best I could?

In the evening, do a mental assessment of your actions for that day. This practice is best done when you are alone and can think clearly. Is there any point in the day you could have acted nicer? Spoken kinder words? Helped someone? Worked harder, or worked less?

Now, recognize one thing you did for someone else. Did you spend time with your children? Help a friend study for a test? Give help to a tourist lost on the street?

Your day is filled with so many opportunities to be of help to people. It is a great way to make a great day.

One of the best ways to continue to grow is by recognizing

your actions, behavior, and goodwill during the day. At the end of each day, and several times during the day, I stop to reflect on my life, goals, purpose, and the direction I'm heading in.

This daily habit could have a significant impact on your life if you do it at least once a day. You can reflect on your day and life while watching the sunset or while eating dinner with your family.

Perform this deep analysis of your time spent and you will become better at who you are, more proactive in your day-to-day life, and be more productive in your work and at home.

Before you go to bed, make a promise to yourself: **Tomorrow will be a better day than today** (even if today was great!). If you stay fixed on this attitude, all of your days will be amazing.

It will be better because you will try harder to make a better day by helping people, listening, and doing everything possible to grow.

Take a pen and paper and write down three things you did today. Did you:

- Work on a project?
- Help another person?
- Spend time with a friend or family?
- Exercise?
- Read a book?
- Work on developing a new habit?

Action Prompt: Reflect on Your Day!

- Make a list of actions or activities you want to do each day or week. You can review this just before bed or after dinner. This could be the best time of the day to reflect on what

you can improve for tomorrow.
- You can reflect on your work, relationships, hobbies, and recognize those areas that can be improved. Make a note of what you should stop doing.
- Look at your life from a big picture perspective and note anything you can try differently to improve and make a difference.

CHAPTER 44

FOCUS ON THE PRESENT MOMENT

*"Doing the best at this moment puts you
in the best place for the next moment."*

—Oprah Winfrey

Many people expend mental energy worrying about tomorrow, about the future, or they obsess about what they could have done differently yesterday in the past. This creates regret and can lead to a deeper level of negative thinking. If you keep your mind in the present day and moment, you give up the obsession to change yesterday.

You can't change the decisions made in the past, even if it was ten minutes ago, but you can live in the now and make sound choices in this moment.

Too often, we try to predict the future and expend lots of energy worrying about whether everything will work out. Will I have enough money? Will I be happy? Is my job going to be secure until I retire? How much time do I have left?

The future is not certain, and there are no guarantees or promises. These thoughts just go around in your mind without any real answers. Your life would be much more peaceful if you train your thoughts and mind to stay in the now.

You could plan for the best and experience the worst. Or plan for the worst and get the best. You don't know what is going to happen in five, ten, or twenty years from today. Everything could be totally different when you wake up tomorrow.

Do your best to let go of the future fears and bring everything back to the only moment that matters: Now.

A mentor once told me: *"One thing in life is certain, and that is that nothing is certain. You control the moment and how you choose to live right now with what you have. That's all anyone has."*

If you stay focused on events beyond your control, you will continue to defeat yourself. Focus on what you can manage, and that is always the present moment. In this moment, living in the now, you can create the tomorrow you want.

The only way to know what is happening tomorrow is by creating it in the present moment. How you live now is setting up your future habits and behaviors.

Stay in the now and you will experience a greater sense of peace, less stress, and eliminate future worry all at the same time.

Action Prompt: Live in the Present Moment!

- **Concentrate on your one task.** If you are drinking coffee, think about the coffee. If you are cooking, stay focused on the food in your kitchen. Your thoughts will run away. Let them go and bring your mind back to the activity in front of you.
- **Focus on breathing.** Breathe in, hold it for four seconds, and breathe out to a count of four. Perform this exercise five times. Take a break. Do it again.

- **Visualize your daily goal**: What is the one goal you are focused on today? Visualize working on this goal. The steps you are taking one after the other that brings you closer to completing it.

CHAPTER 45

SAY NO TO 90% OF EVERYTHING

*"The question isn't who is going to let me;
it's who is going to stop me."*

— Ayn Rand

Saying "Yes" to everything puts you in a difficult position. First of all, if you say YES to everything asked of you, people will expect a YES every time. You'll be expected to give in and say YES to everything.

If you are a YES person, you could be a people-pleaser. You always try to do the right thing for your family, your manager, and your friends so that you don't disappoint them. You soon find yourself saying yes to complete strangers you don't even know. Next, you get labeled as the person who will do anything because you try so hard to make everyone happy.

Everyone but you, that is.

When you say YES to something, you're saying NO to something else. For example, you say YES when:

- Your boss asks you to stay late for the third time this week. But this means saying NO to spending time with your children.
- Your co-worker asks you to help them with a report.

But saying NO means you're not getting your own work done on time.
- A friend asks you for a loan of $50. But this means saying NO to having money for the weekend.

You might be helping someone out, but your compliance to do everything makes you a people-pleaser. And nobody has respect for a doormat. This is especially true if you're in the habit of saying YES, but inside, you really mean NO. Now you're temporarily pleasing others and disappointing yourself for not being strong enough.

You don't have to say NO all the time, but strive for 90%. It's up to you how often you agree to do something, but the trigger to be aware of is when you say YES and really mean NO.

Say NO when:

- Your schedule is too busy to accommodate a request.
- You have other plans that a YES would interfere with.
- You don't have the resources to say YES (e.g. time and money).
- You need to relax after a long, hard day.

Action Prompt: Say NO to 90% of everything!

Start taking score and add up the number of times you say YES when you really wanted to say NO? Is there a specific situation this happens? Or talking with one person in particular? By identifying the situation or person, you can reveal the fears that prompt you to give in and say YES instead of NO.

CHAPTER 46

PLAN YOUR FINANCIAL FREEDOM

"Stop chasing the money and start chasing the passion."

— Tony Hsieh

The freedom to live your life without financial burden is what many people dream of but few are able to achieve. If you want to truly succeed in life, having a plan for financial success is the path to build.

With a time investment of just one hour, you could have a plan for your financial future that is targeted towards helping you achieve financial freedom.

Why do over half the people who work for sixty years end up with no money towards retirement age? Although the reasons are different for everyone, the #1 reason amongst the majority is that they **fail to plan**.

If you **fail to plan, you are planning to fail**.

When it comes to planning your financial freedom, you have to begin somewhere. It doesn't matter if your age is twenty or fifty, you must begin with something. If you always think it's too late to begin, you'll be left working until you're eighty-five, if you are even healthy enough to work.

Financial planning is just that: A plan to be financially free at a specific age so you no longer live with the worry of dying broke. Or worse, working up to your last dying breath.

There are many people who don't plan for the future when it comes to saving cash. They keep waiting until they make more money, get a better job, or the economy improves before doing something. It doesn't matter the situation you are in or the state of the economy. Financial

planning is something you need to always be thinking about and working towards.

Do you have a plan for your financial future? Here are eight strategies that will help you to become successful with your finances:

1. **Save 10% of your salary every month.** Yes, no matter how much you earn, you must pay yourself first before anyone else gets paid. This means putting 10-20% in your savings account every month before you pay your bills.
2. **Avoid buying stuff you don't need.** Most of the things people spend money on are worthless. Clothes that are worn once, books on the shelf that are never read, or an expensive car that costs you money from the first day you buy it. Be aware of what you really need. Buy only the essentials, and save your extra cash. Everything you buy, you eventually have to get rid of.
3. **Learn about saving, debt, and investment.** Teach yourself everything you can about what it means to be financially free. There are many books out there and people you can hire to teach you all you need.

    One of the biggest reasons we fail financially is from a lack of understanding. They don't teach financial management in most schools. You need to teach yourself—and the sooner the better.

4. **Take responsibility for your financial future.** Trusting someone else to take care of your future finances is a mistake. You can only trust in your own judgment. This means taking responsibility by deciding to set yourself up for success. Nobody cares more about your money than you do.
5. **Set financial goals.** The next best reason we fail at finances is due to no goal planning. You can't hit a financial target if you don't know what it is. Make a clear plan with goals for setting your financial targets.
6. **Pay with cash only.** If you don't have the cash, put off making a purchase until you do. You will experience a deeper level of satisfaction that you applied personal discipline toward saving the money rather than just paying for it with a card and spending money you don't yet have. The belief that you can own it now and pay later is ruining your chances of financial freedom.
7. **Track your expenses.** By tracking your daily expenses for everything you spend money on, it empowers you with knowing where your hard-earned cash is going. Keep a daily/weekly/monthly expenses journal. You can update this at the end of each day.
8. **Eliminate your debt!** From today, write down everything you are spending. Do this for 30 days. This practice will give you a clear indication of how much extra money you spend each month. Then after 30 days, review what you have spent.

Action Prompt: Plan for Financial Freedom!

- Study the eight strategies for financial freedom and take one action this week. Will you begin by teaching yourself

about finances? Are you going to visit an investment bank to discuss this with a professional? Can you write down your financial goals for the next 1-3 years?
- Decide what you can stop buying and try to reduce the amount you spend. After one year, you will be amazed. You should see a significant increase in the money you have instead of the money you owe in debt.

CHAPTER 47

LIVE WITH PURPOSE AND CLARITY

> *"When you discover your mission, you will feel its demand. It will fill you with enthusiasm and a burning desire to get to work on it."*
>
> —W. Clement Stone

You are brought into this world with a unique call to action. It is a personal mission that calls for a deeper expression of the life you have been gifted to lead.

Make it your mission to integrate this passion into everything you do. What you focus on is what you become. What you take intentional action towards defines your greater purpose. The thoughts and dreams that keep you awake at night are directing you to move towards this higher purpose at all times.

So, what do you think about all day long?

Focus on performing the right actions and you'll do the right thing. Allow nothing to pull you off course, and when it does, you will have the focus and clarity to correct your course. You are, at all times, the *master of fate* **in control of your own** *life vessel*.

Focus on the now and make today count. By staying in

the present, you are in a stronger position to connect with your purpose. Make a firm decision about what you want to accomplish, the values you are choosing to live by, and the principles to guide you to where you need to be.

Finally, focus all your attention on achieving whatever would have the greatest impact on what matters most to you and the people touched by your purpose and passion.

Ask yourself, "Am I fulfilling my life's purpose right now?"

Don't worry if it feels like you're lost. Everyone finds their purpose through experiencing life in many ways. Try new things and if they don't fit, keep searching until you discover your ultimate passion.

Don't live below your potential. Don't settle for what is "good enough". Instead, push yourself to rise above self-created limitations. Question the voices of doubt and challenge yourself to follow your path.

Whatever it is that is calling to you now, I encourage you to move towards it. Embrace this passion and pursue it with everything you've got. You must learn to live creatively by designing a dream for your life that fully expresses who you are and why you are here.

A life lived with purpose is the most powerful and fulfilling life of all.

Action Prompt: Live with Purpose and Clarity!

Ask yourself these questions for clarity around your purpose:

- Is the work I'm doing fulfilling my purpose or just paying the bills?
- If I could be and do anything in this world, what would that life look like?

- Do I have a vision for my life? Where do I want to be emotionally, spiritually, and financially in the next ten years?

CHAPTER 48

BECOME A SUCCESSFUL MINIMALIST

"We think we can't become a minimalist until our lives have settled down. But it's actually the other way around; we won't be able to settle down until we're living a minimalist life."

—Fumio Sasaki

Minimalism is the practice of wanting less and getting rid of your accumulated possessions. The minimalist focuses on life experiences and enjoys the finer things in life that don't cost money.

Minimalism is the intentional attention we pay to the things we hold most valuable, while removing the distractions that take us away from living the minimalist lifestyle.

There are 5 key benefits of practicing the minimalism lifestyle:

1. **Reduced stress** because you're not constantly in pursuit of things.
2. **Less living space required**. With a minimalist lifestyle, less room is needed for the things we acquire. This adds to a cleaner space and also reduces the need to be cleaning around things.
3. **Improved focus**. With less stress and less stuff, you

experience an increase in focus. This adds to your intentional purpose as you breathe minimalism into your life.
4. **Live with intention and purpose**. This is the deepest reason to become a minimalist. A life that is lived with intentional reason and focus.
5. **Freedom.** We become attached to possessions and build a false sense of self-worth by what we own. You can be true and genuine while living a life of freedom with less to collect and worry about keeping.

Becoming a minimalist will give you more time, energy, and will free up more of your money. It's that journey of intentional self-improvement, and appreciating what we already have, that will bring us the **contentment** we seek. We must stay focused on gratitude in order to get the results we want.

Here are **7 simple steps** you can start with to build your minimalist lifestyle:

1. You can begin the minimalist lifestyle by getting rid of stuff in your home. Sell it, recycle it, or give it away.
2. Start with each room and move through your house, decluttering as you go.
3. Take old clothes to the used clothing shops. Take your books to libraries or used book stores.
4. Minimalize your workspace. Identify clutter and get rid of it.
5. Focus on only one thing at a time and eliminate multi-tasking.
6. Maintain a simple diet and do more cooking at home.
7. Set up a savings plan for becoming debt free and strive for the freedom of having less stuff with more cash in the bank.

Action Prompt: Become a Minimalist!

- Becoming a minimalist is a choice you make. You can begin by getting rid of stuff around your home or office.
- Clean out the garage, your upstairs living space and closets. Stop buying stuff online you don't need. By reducing clutter, you reduce living a complex lifestyle and adopt the minimalist approach.
- For a thorough walk through of becoming a minimalist and getting rid of clutter, I recommend you read 10-Minute Declutter: The Stress-Free Habit for Simplifying Your Home by S.J. Scott and Barrie Davenport.

CHAPTER 49

EMBRACE THE FEAR OF RISK

"Success seems to be connected with action. Successful people keep moving. They make mistakes, but they don't quit."

—Conrad Hilton

What challenge would you try if you knew that you absolutely couldn't fail? What risks would you take if you were guaranteed to win?

You are taking a risk every day when you are not taking the risks necessary to change. You are in a relationship that makes you miserable, but you are afraid to change it. Why? You might not find anyone else.

You want to quit your job so you can do what you love, but you are afraid to start. Why? Your job is secure and brings in a full-time paycheck—at the cost of your happiness.

When it comes to risk, there are two sides to every perspective. Many people see risk as dangerous. You take a chance and put your life savings into an investment that could fail. You quit your job to start a new venture. You decide to try something new that many have never attempted before. Why do we do these things and take such chances knowing what the odds are?

We avoid taking risks, no matter how small, because we

want to keep what we have. "I'll do it someday when I'm ready," you say. "I'll do it when I have enough time, enough resources, or enough confidence."

If you are still wishing for that perfect day to arrive when it will all be in your favor, you'll be waiting a long time. The only day that matters is today, and the only time you have is now. So, are you ready to take this day and do something great with it? Can you visualize where you will be six months from now if you make a change? For the people who are prepared to accept the risk, the fear of not succeeding is stronger than the fear of failing. It is so strong that the risk is worth it.

Moving towards risk is a shift in your attitude. When you catch yourself making excuses about why you shouldn't do something, challenge the thoughts that are stopping you from taking intentional action. Remember: You always risk failure, not because of what you tried and failed at but, because of what you didn't try in the first place.

Your life is at risk every moment of the day. It could all end today. And if it does, you want to be there, ready to say that you did everything in this life to make it the best you could. You want to be able to say that failure never held you back, and even when you were scared, in those moments of fear and doubt and uncertainty, you ignored the fear and made it happen anyway.

Action Prompt: Embrace the Fear of Risk!

Here are 3 simple strategies you can implement now to make risk-taking fun, challenging, and less scary:

1. **Set a challenging goal. Make your biggest goal a risk. Take an impossible-to-achieve goal this year and challenge yourself to achieve it.**

2. **Set big goals**. When it comes to your goal challenge, be bold. Go with courage and set a goal for yourself that seems absolutely ridiculous. You can only fail if you do nothing.
3. **Defeat the resistance of taking risks.** When you challenge something new without knowing the outcome, there is always resistance. You consider giving up when the fear becomes too strong. But when the risk is worth the reward, you can beat resistance. Be the risk-taker that other people want to model for success.
4. Identify one thing you have been procrastinating on because the risk scares you. Ask yourself, "What is the one immediate step I can take right now?"

CHAPTER 50

BECOME AN UNDEFEATED CHAMPION

*"The difference between a successful person and others
is not a lack of strength, not a lack of knowledge,
but rather a lack of will."*

—Vince Lombardi

To become an undefeated champion, you must acknowledge the challenges standing between you and everything you have ever dreamed of. When something is in the way, you must find a way to remove it.

You are stronger than you realize. When adversity defeats you, it isn't the end of the fight. It is just the beginning. Deciding to remain undefeated means fighting through rejection, job loss, bankruptcy, or losing everything you own.

When defeat is pushing you down and all the odds are stacked against you, what will you do? When everything hangs in the balance, will you react out of fear? Or will you take a proactive approach and do something about it?

To rebound from a major loss or setback, you have to let go of the potential losses and focus on your future gains. By taking immediate action in the face of fear, you are programming your mind to handle adversity and failure. **Failure is the path to**

victory. Losing tests your resilience by challenging you to rise to the problem instead of running away.

You have to stay committed in your resolve to see this through to the end. You have to weigh the risks of what might happen if you keep failing, and what you stand to lose if you give up and give in to defeat.

Here are three examples of champions who proved they are undefeatable:

Abraham Lincoln suffered incredible loss and defeat in his life before he became the 16th President of the United States in 1861. His wife and child died. He lost the presidential election several times before winning. Only his resilience to push through to the end is what makes his story so incredible.

J.K. Rowling's dream was to be a writer. She was so passionate about her stories that she would spend time at work writing *Harry Potter*. She got fired from her job because she was writing her book during working hours.

J.K. Rowling was on welfare and almost homeless when she continued to write *Harry Potter and the Philosopher's Stone*. The Harry Potter series has now sold over 450 million copies.

Walt Disney was fired from his job as an animator for the *Kansas City Star* newspaper. The reason was his editor thought he lacked imagination and creativity, and he had no good ideas.

Walt Disney and his brother (Roy Disney) then set up the Disney Brothers Studio, where they created the classic animated films that went on to win 22 Academy Awards.

What is the #1 action you can take right now that will

move you in the right direction? Then, what is the next action after that?

Continue to list out your action plan that moves you closer towards your goals and becoming an undefeated champion.

Action Prompt: Become an Undefeated Champion!

Think about these questions and write out your answers:

- What tough decisions can you make right now that would change everything for you?
- What are you willing to give up in order to become an undefeated champion?
- What is the biggest fear holding your back? The fear of vulnerability, losing something, or failing to gain what you want?

"There is never just one thing that leads to success for anyone. I feel it is always a combination of passion, dedication, hard work, and being in the right place at the right time."

—Lauren Conrad

CHAPTER 51

TAKE THE DIFFICULT PATH

"The successful warrior is the average man, with laser-like focus."

—Bruce Lee

You must choose to take the difficult path in life if you're going to overcome the obstacles holding you back. There is great satisfaction gained in doing the hard things.

You feel the thrill of possibility when you decide to tackle a difficult challenge. There's a chance of achieving something wonderful. Even if you fail, the lessons prove invaluable. Taking the hard way expands your imagination and makes you question all of your thoughts about limitations.

The great thing about taking the difficult path and facing challenging obstacles is that when you succeed at winning over one obstacle, you know you can conquer another.

Walking the difficult path is about challenging all your limitations. You accept only the best from your efforts. You are willing to fail and try again until you succeed.

For example:

- Running a full marathon.
- Writing a full-length novel.

- Moving across the country (or to a new country) for better opportunities.
- Making a decision to quit your job and try something new.
- Start up your own business.

People learn to fear life less by doing the things they fear the most. If there was an easier way, I'd give it to you. Don't fall for quick wins that are easy. There is no easy way to real success. If it's easy, then you haven't succeeded. You settled for what you could get.

Ask yourself: *"Where will I be in one year from now if I continue investing time and energy in all the wrong activities?"*

I can tell you the answer. You'll be doing the same things years from now and regretting not doing what you could have done to make all the difference.

The difficult path takes daily discipline, but the reward comes later. The easy way gives you an instant reward, but you suffer for it later.

Visualize where you'll be in one year, one month, or next week if you do what's difficult *now*. Think about the difference you'll make, not just in your own life but in the lives of the people you could help. There's no better way to live than doing what you love and doing it well.

How will you decide to live your life? Will you take the easy way or the hard way?

Action Prompt: Take the Difficult Path!

- Open up and observe what you fear.
- Let the fear in. Open the window to your soul and accept your fear as a necessary entity. What's the worst that can happen?

- Think about all the days you've lived in fear of doing the things that you really wanted to do. Has any of the stuff that you thought would be so bad really happened?
- Visualize your life at the end. See yourself as having overcome the obstacles and fears that held you back. See yourself tackling your greatest adversary and winning. Imagine what it will be like when you can look back on your life with a feeling of triumph that your journey was well-lived.

CHAPTER 52

PERSEVERE AND GO THE EXTRA MILE

"Patience, persistence and perspiration make an unbeatable combination for success."

—Napoleon Hill

Your commitment to going the extra mile means you are prepared to do **whatever it takes** to succeed. You train harder, work harder, stay awake longer, and push past the challenges of resistance. Going the extra mile is about defeating expectations by over-delivering on performance.

You are committed to pushing yourself further every day by breaking those tough mental and physical obstacles.

Successful achievers dedicated to this path push harder than anyone else. They ignore weak excuses and never complain about the "extra work" required to achieve the goal. The value in this discipline is realized when you are the last one standing at the end of the race.

You must be willing to break the fears of your mind. You have unlimited potential for living a life of greatness. Many people fail to believe in what they can achieve, and so, they fail to become everything they have always wanted. You are always willing to do whatever it takes to succeed.

Through pushing forward with perseverance and determination, you discipline your mind to become a rock instead of a cushion.

By going the extra mile, you are:

- The author who writes just one more book after the previous five have failed.
- The entrepreneur who takes a chance on one more business opportunity with the last dollar they have.
- The runner who pushes towards the last mile in the race when most have given up.

What are you prepared to do to go that extra mile? Would you:

- Give up your weekends for the next year to work on your hustle when everyone else is relaxing and enjoying the weekend?
- Throw your TV away because it's a distraction to the work you're doing?
- Stay an hour late after work to help your manager when everyone else has gone home?
- Wake up one hour earlier when the rest of the world is sleeping?
- Train for two hours longer than the strongest person on your sports team?

Action Prompt: Persevere and Go the Extra Mile!

- Be the one who goes the extra mile in everything you do. Take immediate action when the moment calls for it and you will never fall into the habit of procrastination again.
- Build your confidence and discover new opportunities by

rendering the best in service and trust. Going the extra mile is a value you can adopt as your #1 success trait.

CHAPTER 53

VISUALIZE YOUR FUTURE POSSIBILITIES

"If you don't design your own life plan, chances
are you'll fall into someone else's plan.
And guess what they have planned
for you? Not much.

—Jim Rohn

One of the most powerful strategies for developing self-confidence and creating the life you want is mentally rehearsing the steps required to get you there. This is how concentrated visualization plays an important role in your success. And having no vision for your life can result in your lack of success, too.

When you can map out life's journey in your imagination, you are mentally rehearsing the actions needed to move straight to your goal. By focusing on your vision of how you want your life to be, you begin to attract the people and circumstances to help you get there.

By tapping into the creativity of your unlimited imagination, the forces of the universe go to work to grant you all the things you can imagine. The life we create through visual imagery is a preview of what's to come.

Visualizing the life you intend to lead is setting up all future actions to pivot toward making it happen. You are not just visualizing what you want to achieve but, how you are going to get there.

Without a vision of what you want, you will always be at the mercy of circumstances created by external events. But with your plan firmly in your mind, you can be confident that the road you're on is the right one. Every great success story began with an idea, a vision, and a plan of action that consisted of concrete steps.

Visualization makes all possibilities endless. Here are the 6 steps you can implement today to start building your vision.

1. First, **know exactly what you want**—and determine what you have to do to get it!
2. **Embrace your vision**. When you see the object of your desire, hold it in your mind until it develops into a crystal-clear image of what it is you're going after.
3. **Feed your imagination** every day. Develop your vision of the life you want and pursue it relentlessly until it's yours. Don't stop thinking about it until it materializes. Focus, persist, and push your imagination to the brink of mental exhaustion.
4. Think **positive thoughts** and utilize clear, intense emotions. Be passionate about your vision and you will develop the ability to manifest what you desire.
5. **Believe in your vision.** You must have complete faith in the visual imagination of your dreams. Erase all doubt and use affirmations to build a foundation of faith and positive energy. People who doubt the power they have within eventually fail to produce the results they want.

6. **Choose the goal** you feel most passionate about. Imagine the action steps you would need to take in order to reach this goal. How would you turn your vision into a reality? This is the stage where you mentally rehearse the steps you're taking to get to the inevitable outcome.

Action Prompt: Visualize Your Future Possibilities!

- Everything begins with a vision. Set aside time every day to weave your thoughts and images together. Fill your imagination with all the things you can visualize doing, having and being.
- Let nothing pull your vision away from your dream. Stay fixed on the ultimate outcome, and align all your actions with your vision.
- Share your vision with an accountability partner, mentor, or mastermind community.

CHAPTER 54

PUSH HARD WHEN YOU ENCOUNTER RESISTANCE

"Don't wait until everything is just right. It will never be perfect. There will always be challenges, obstacles and less than perfect conditions. So what. Get started now. With each step you take, you will grow stronger and stronger, more and more skilled, more and more self-confident and more and more successful.

—Mark Victor Hansen

How many people do you know that start something and soon give up after a few days?

They start to play a new sport but give up if they haven't turned pro in the first three months. They take up painting but drop it after the first attempt because it doesn't look like a Picasso. They leave a sales position after the first day when nobody buys anything on the first twenty calls. Or they quit the gym after three months because the weight they tried lose is the same as when they joined.

One fact is true about success: it's not an overnight event. Everyone starts with that first step.

Success takes time, practice, patience, and a level of

persistent action and resilience before you see results. If you want to break through the resistance, you must be willing to do whatever it takes.

The hard way *is* the way when it comes to handling challenges such as fear, criticism, and rejection.

When you are dedicated to the path of failing forward fast, every step carries you closer to your objective. If you get stuck, take time out to assess where you're at and take immediate action when you're clear on your plan.

If you stumble, get up again. When you fail at something for the 100th time, look at the situation and see what you could do differently. Course correct as you move ahead.

Take it slowly if you must. It isn't a race. In many cases, overnight success is the culmination of five, ten, or twenty years of consistent work. But you have to continuously push harder when you encounter resistance.

Every challenge is met with a level of resistance before you hit that success mark. You can persevere through any challenge by following these 3 steps:

1. Stay committed to your actions for the long-term. You have to work at something for a long time before you gather enough momentum to master it.
2. Define your plan. If resistance is strong, go back to your purpose and define your plan. Be clear about what you're working towards.
3. Maintain high energy levels. Eat healthily, exercise, and practice meditation to maintain your mindset. This is key. If your mind is not focused and is weak on energy, you will fail.

Action Prompt: Push Hard When You Encounter Resistance

- You will meet with resistance when your objective is worthy of the struggle. Anything easily obtained is rarely valued. The champions who break through meet resistance head-on and figure out how to break through it.
- To persevere, stay committed to your objective, push hard through difficult times, and develop a detailed vision for the life you want to lead.

CHAPTER 55

REJECTION IS THE BEST LEARNING EXPERIENCE

"Our greatest fear should not be of failure ... but of succeeding at things in life that don't really matter."

—Francis Chan

Rejection is a dominating force. It impacts everyone's confidence to a certain degree.

Let's look at an example of how rejection works in one of two ways. Two women both work for a sales company. They are both given a challenge to knock on a hundred doors. The challenge is: Don't stop knocking until you've hit all one hundred homes.

One of the women starts strong, and she actually has eleven sales out of twenty-five homes. But then her streak wanes and, at the last twenty- five homes, she gets rejected again and again. Feeling like a failure, she eventually quits and goes home.

The other woman hits all one hundred homes. But she doesn't hit a single sale until house #93. She was rejected by 92 customers before she sold her first product. Then, she continued on to the rest of the homes, completing her target of all one-hundred homes. But, in total, she still only sold one product.

When the president of the company heard about this, he nominated the woman for the employee of the month, not based on the amount of sales but her commitment to perseverance. In spite of the rejection received, she pushed forward, rejection after rejection, until she got that first win.

When asked how she pushed on with so many people rejecting her sales pitch, she said, "They aren't rejecting me. They are saying no to the product. They don't even see the salesperson. At least, that's how I perceive it."

She also said, "Most salespeople take NO personally, but when someone walks onto your property looking to spend money, you are just making the introduction. They are not 'buying a salesperson,' they either want your product or they don't."

To push ahead and achieve your final goal, you must be ready for rejection. It will happen. But the difference is in how you perceive this rejection. Will you let it defeat you, or can you push ahead no matter what?

Rejection is a state of mind. It is your attitude that determines if you win or lose. Everyone gets rejected hundreds of times in their lifetime. Many run and try to avoid rejection from happening. But the successful person takes that rejection and uses it to create opportunity.

People who fail always hide from rejection. They take the easy way to success by accepting what they can get instead of what they really want.

Rejection is your opportunity to try again, only doing it better the next time. And if you are rejected again, you keep trying. Keep going until you start getting more people saying YES instead of NO.

Action Prompt: Rejection is the Best Learning Experience!

- Rejection is a game you have to play until you succeed. If you give up after the first few people say NO, you will continue to lose. You must get rejected to get over rejection.
- Make it a habit to get rejected as many times as possible. Instead of fearing rejection, look forward to it and accept it when it comes. Instead of running away from it, run towards it.
- Keep track of and count the number of times you are rejected. Compare the amount of rejections you get and see each rejection as a win.

CHAPTER 56

CRUSH THE OBSTACLES IN YOUR WAY

"The best people possess a feeling for beauty, the courage to take risks, the discipline to tell the truth, the capacity for sacrifice. Ironically, their virtues make them vulnerable; they are often wounded, sometimes destroyed."

—Ernest Hemingway

Obstacles are barriers that stand between you and the fulfillment of your dreams. To make consistent progress and get to where you want to be in five or ten years, you'll have to face life's challenging roadblocks along the way.

These are the obstacles that show up in your life and can throw your plans out of order. Your success in any situation is measured by your performance in working through these challenges as they show up.

The obstacles I'm referring to here include losing a job, getting a divorce, physical or mental health issues, disagreements with business partners, difficult family relationships or difficult decisions, and personal trauma blocking you from making key decisions.

Life's obstacles present an opportunity to strengthen yourself and become more confident as you defeat your own limitations. One of the greatest measures of successful people is their ability to transcend life's difficulties and overcome the roadblocks that threaten to hold them back. Successful people stand up to challenges that threaten their goals and dreams.

When confronted with a problem that seems too big to conquer, you can find a way to overcome it by using the simple **six-step process** below:

1. **Identify the obstacle.** Do you want to buy a house but you don't have enough money? Do you have to speak to your boss about a problem with your work? No matter what the situation is, the first step to working toward a solution is to identify it. Write it out on paper to make it real. Then, once you have identified the problem....
2. **Create a list of possible solutions.** Now that you have clearly defined the obstacle, it is easier to draw ideas on what actions to take. For the second step, create a list of possible solutions. By putting your ideas to paper, you can see with greater clarity the solution to overcoming your obstacles.
3. **Select the best choice.** Next, from the list of options, choose the best one. Write down the best solution and work toward taking immediate action. Prioritize the options in order of importance.
4. **Take Immediate Action.** It's time to act. Take one action step towards this obstacle. What do you have to do? Call someone? Research information? Whatever it is, do it now.
5. **Follow up on the outcome.** After applying the formula to your situation, you may not have an immediate outcome. The application of your solutions may take time to work. The final stage is to follow up on the results. Did you get the outcome you wanted? Did you experience a different result than what you expected?

6. **Try Again:** If you didn't get what you were hoping for, continue to apply other solutions. Just because something didn't deliver the first time doesn't mean the situation is hopeless. For every obstacle you face, there is a way to overcome it.

Action Prompt: Crush the Obstacles in Your Way!

- What obstacles are holding you back right now? Do you have a plan for getting past them? Write down the #1 roadblock for you today.
- Visualize what your life would look like after you have conquered this problem. How would things be different? How would you feel? Spend 20 minutes every evening imagining this scenario.
- **Apply the 6-step formula** described above to help you develop a concrete action plan.

CHAPTER 57

BEAT THE PROCRASTINATION HABIT!

"Procrastination is the fear of success. People procrastinate because they are afraid of the success that they know will result if they move ahead now. Because success is heavy, carries a responsibility with it, it is much easier to procrastinate and live on the 'someday I'll' philosophy."

—Denis Waitley

Procrastination—or what I call *task avoidance*—is a defensive technique used to escape from the pain and unpleasantness of having to perform an undesirable task. This is a habit of escape used to get yourself out of doing something that has been linked to your mind as an activity that is boring or not worth your time.

When you procrastinate on doing the important activities that must be done, you put yourself at risk for failing to do the things that need to be done.

We procrastinate on many things: Studying for a test, cleaning the house, filling out medical forms, or in more serious cases, filing tax returns or applying for a business loan. There are many things you can avoid doing, and you might get away with it for a long time, but eventually, everything comes back to you.

Procrastination costs you time, money, and self-esteem. If

continued over many years, the end cost is the life you could have had but never did.

Why do we procrastinate? The four main reasons are:

1. The fear of failing at something.
2. Lack of interest.
3. Lack of motivation.
4. Low self-confidence.

Procrastination defeats you in many ways. It lowers your self-esteem, increases your stress, and makes you feel guilty for postponing something you know should be worked on.

Regardless of why you procrastinate, this negative habit is very damaging to you in the long-term. For this reason, it's recommended that you take consistent action steps to beat your procrastination habit.

Here is a simple 3-step process that I call "Breaking down the procrastination habit."

1. Identify 1 task or job you have been procrastinating about. Write it down on paper.
2. Write down the easiest step you could take right now that moves you forward in starting this work. It could be something as simple as sending a short email or opening a document on your desktop.
3. Do the next simple task.

Action Prompt: Beat the Procrastination Habit!

- It is a natural path we take to avoid unpleasant things. Life is full of things we don't want to do, and activities that we

view as a waste of time but must be done in order to make progress and continue to grow.
- Take care of things as they come up, and if you can't do it right away for lack of information or resources, make sure it gets done when the time is right.

CHAPTER 58

CREATE A "THINGS I HAVE ACCOMPLISHED IN MY LIFETIME" LIST

*"Sometimes carrying on, just carrying on,
is the superhuman achievement."*

—Albert Camus

We are always focused on the next task, the new project, or the current big goal. Driven by productivity and trying to get more done, we lose track of important accomplishments.

We become focused on what is going wrong, the opportunity missed, or the failures that cannot be undone. This train of thought leads to regret and shame for not achieving as much as you had wanted.

You try to make up for this by creating more goals that you struggle to finish. Instead of coming up with more goals to achieve, identify the achievements you have already succeeded at.

Recognize your victories and celebrate the wins you had last week, last month, or ten years ago. You would be surprised by how much you have really accomplished in your lifetime, regardless of whether you are seventy-five or seventeen.

It's not always about winning. If you run in a race but you

don't finish first, you shouldn't disqualify this as a loss. You still participated in the race and that's a win!

Too many times we dismiss our efforts as unimportant if we don't get a trophy or a medal. Success is a matter of perspective and gratitude. Your **small wins matter**.

Make a list of everything that you have accomplished in the last year. Then break it down to the last five years and the big accomplishments you've had in your lifetime. Make a list of at least fifty personal victories. You'll be surprised by how much you've really achieved!

Did you…

- Write a book?
- Graduate from University?
- Get hired by a new company?
- Run in a marathon?
- Earn your black belt?
- Help someone?
- Have a baby?
- Take a family dream vacation?

You are a bigger success than you think. Never think of yourself as less. Appreciate the greatness of this life knowing that you're a big part of it, and you DO matter.

Action Prompt: Track Your Victories!

- Create a list of your achievements.
- Once you have your list, post it where you can see it. You want to keep it visible so that it serves as a reminder that you're doing a lot of things right.
- From this moment forward, pay attention to what you can

achieve today. Track your small wins and write down the goals you accomplish.
- Pass it forward! The biggest accomplishment is in helping other people succeed, and then everyone passes it along!

CHAPTER 59

RAISE YOUR PERSONAL STANDARDS

"You can't please everyone. When you're too focused on living up to other people's standards, you aren't spending enough time raising your own. Some people may whisper, complain and judge. But for the most part, it's all in your head. People care less about your actions than you think. Why? They have their own problems!"

—Kris Carr

Raising your standards means to set expectations for how you are treated in this world. You determine your own value by deciding what you are willing to accept from people, and others will always treat you according to the expectations you set.

For people that show low self-esteem and confidence, they allow themselves to be yelled at, bullied, and put down by people at work or in social gatherings.

You have to raise your standards as high as you can, or the world will lower your standards and treat you without respect. You can take control of your own life by drawing the line on what is acceptable and what you will tolerate.

Remember: It's not the expectations of other people you

should be paying attention to, but the expectations you have set for yourself.

You must turn your "should do" into a "must do." When you must get something done, you push yourself to do it. A "should" get it done becomes a someday goal that rarely gets accomplished.

How do you raise your standards?

Doing the work that is difficult but extremely rewarding. Surrounding yourself with people that have a higher skillset, or make 10x more money.

When you fail, don't lower your standards to match the failure and make yourself feel better. You take your standards to the highest level. When most people say NO, you are saying YES. Where 99% fail and give up, you are the 1% that pushes forward.

You always accept nothing but the absolute best, and your best is better than anyone else can commit to.

Your potential will always reflect your standards. If your standards are average, your efforts will be average. This leads to less-than-average results. You can work 100 hours a week, but if you're working in a job you hate—doing meaningless work—it results in exhaustion and burnout.

Success can only be reached when your standards are raised to a level that scares you.

Identify the fixed beliefs you have about yourself. Put in the work to change these beliefs in time. It won't happen right away, but if you identify your negative beliefs now, you raise personal awareness of what needs to be changed.

You become what you believe, who you spend time with, and the positive (or negative) self-talk you communicate to yourself. You can change your beliefs, spend time with real game winners, and transform your limited self-talk.

Action Prompt: Raise Your Standards!

- Make a list of the behaviors you no longer find acceptable from other people.
- Make a list of behavior you'll never accept from yourself again.
- Commit yourself to becoming great at what you do. Then become the best at what you do, and become better than your best by aiming for mastery in your field.

CHAPTER 60

GROW YOUR GRIT

"There haven't been genetic studies on grit, but we often think that challenge is inherited but grit is learned. That's not what science says. Science says grit comes from both nature and nurture."

—Angela Duckworth

Grit is the difference between people who talk about doing it, and those that take intentional action and get the results they want. It is your ability to persevere through the roughest conditions imaginable and beat the odds stacked against you. Grit is a mental attitude that doesn't tolerate giving up.

Grit is effort applied over and over again to a skill you are constantly developing. Skill alone isn't enough; you must feed your motivation propelled with a grit-driven attitude for real success to happen.

Grit isn't a trait you are born with. It's a trait you can grow and develop. But you need passion to fuel the fire. Without passion for living and doing what you love, grit will cease to exist.

It is the magic of sticking with your long-term goals through the worst periods of your life. And tapping into your life's passion so you keep going despite the adversity and hardship.

People who have strong levels of grit are immune to defeat. Grit is developed by making the decision to become the best at something, and then working like crazy to succeed at it.

You should build grit into everything you do.

- Grit and determination is what propelled Oprah Winfrey to succeed as one of the most successful talk show celebrities in history.
- Grit and perseverance propelled J.K. Rowling to write and publish her Harry Potter series after the first book was rejected twelve times.
- Grit is what Henry Ford possessed because it pushed him through bankruptcy five times before the Ford Motor Company succeeded.

Grit is the long-term effort you dedicate to getting your goals finished and pushing hard to the finish line. It's a combination of passion and perseverance, and the unbroken belief that failure can be overcome. It's a willingness to conquer life's challenges, and a commitment to do whatever it takes to succeed.

Grit is the difference between people who talk about doing it, and those that take intentional action and get the results they want.

When it comes to success, grit isn't a recommended component to succeed—it's a necessity. Nobody makes it without knowing first what they want. Then, deciding what they are willing to do to get it.

Thomas Edison once said that "Many of life's failures are people who did not realize how close they were to success when they gave up."

How do you develop grit?

Here are 4 strategies you can implement from today to grow your grit and take success from a dream to reality.

1. **Practice your craft.** Grit is driven by what you love to do. If you love to fix things, fix it. If your passion is building things, build it. But turn your desires into action. Practice makes progress, and the more success you have from doing what you love, the stronger grit grows.
2. **Make friends with grit-driven people.** My mentor once said to me, "You can't fly with the eagles if you're hanging out with the turkeys."

    The people you spend the most time with influence your thoughts, feelings and actions. They want you to soar high and become everything you were made to be. You need grit-driven people to push, praise and challenge you.
3. **Create an impossible goal**…and then work hard to make it reality. You'll only succeed if you aim for a goal that scares you. You are in competition with yourself to become better today than yesterday, and to make tomorrow a greater day than today. It's the ongoing pursuit of excellence that gets the prize. Pursue your #1 goal with a vengeance, slay the naysayers, and keep pushing forward.
4. **Pay the price to succeed. Determine the price you are willing to pay** to become better, faster, stronger…and you will have defined your grit by the determination to succeed. Fill your day with the habits needed to develop this mental toughness.

Never give up when the dream is so close. Your mental attitude and commitment to living a life of greatness defines you.

Action Prompt: Grow Your Grit!

Define what grit means for you.

- Is it pushing past that last mile of the race when everyone else has stopped?
- Working one more hour on the basketball court when the rest of the team has hit the showers?
- Writing one more page of your book even after your mind has reached exhaustion?

CONCLUSION

LIVE YOUR BEST LIFE!

"A hero is an ordinary individual who finds the strength to persevere and endure in spite of overwhelming obstacles."

—Christopher Reeve

You made it! I hope you enjoyed the book and can use these strategies throughout your days, weeks, and life ahead. There are many tactics in this book, so take it one step at a time.

Life is always moving forward, even when it feels like nothing is changing. Time is your most valuable resource and you have to use it well. Don't wait for the perfect time or circumstances before taking intentional action and putting these life-changing strategies into practice.

You can only grow when you live your life differently. This means doing things that are uncomfortable, but once it becomes a part of your lifestyle habits, the opportunities you dream about will begin to appear for you.

The best time to live your life fully is NOW. Tomorrow might never arrive, and if it does, you have another chance to give it your best, to learn, and to share your knowledge and lessons learned with friends and family.

Do the things you've always dreamed of doing. Do them

today. Do them again tomorrow. There will come a day when we have no more time, and by then, it's too late.

You owe it to yourself to live the best life you can. If you don't live it, who will? Make your own choices and create your destiny through the power of decision.

Concentrate on the present moment. Bring your past and future together into the present that is happening now. Do one thing today—just one— that starts you towards your journey of living a great life.

We all deserve to have a life that matters, and the only person who can guide you towards that destination is you.

You're the captain of your own ship. Now put both hands on the wheel and point your vessel of life towards the great unknown.

I wish you all the best on your journey, and that your days are filled with all the best this life has to offer...

Scott Allan

> *"The price of success is hard work, dedication to the job at hand, and the determination that whether we win or lose, we have applied the best of ourselves to the task at hand."*
>
> —Vince Lombardi

REDUCE YOUR WORRY HABIT

If you observe your own thinking and how your mind interacts with the world, you become a passenger on a wild ride through a theme park. You can be a witness to all the noise and mayhem that comes with a polluted mind that won't stay in the moment.

People are constantly dealing with their thoughts that focus on "getting" and "having" and "becoming." We are attached to owning something or attached to becoming something.

When things are not going as planned, your mind flips into worry mode. Worry is always grounded in the fear of the future. Worrisome thoughts are thoughts we give permission to take control of our state of mind. We worry when we lack trust or faith.

If faith is the belief that things will work out, worry is the belief that everything is in danger of falling apart. It won't work out. You could fail. This could happen or that could happen. Your thoughts start to play out the worst-case scenarios of a bad outcome that results in you ending up empty handed, broke, or alone.

Worry is a broken loop of fear. This is a daily struggle with the mind. You want to trust in something bigger than yourself, but you can't. So, how can you fight back against the loop of fear that worry creates? How do you stop worrying about the future "possibilities" and start living?

You'll need to bring yourself back to the present moment.

It starts with reframing your situation and life in a positive framework. Are you seeing the world as a scary, frightful place? Are you afraid of waking up and finding yourself homeless one day? Do you think you'll lose your job next week?

Well, all these things could happen—or none of them could happen. The extent to which they happen is up to you. Most of the worst things that will ever happen to you take place in your mind first... and that's it! Think about the grand symphony of chaos that is constantly conducted inside your mind. But you, as the conductor of your thoughts, can choose how and what to think about. Imagine that. You are the master of your own mind. Remind yourself of this fact and take time to observe your thoughts.

We always have ideas, voices and opinions, mixed with conflicting thoughts based on information we are not entirely sure is correct. How do you separate the good from the bad? How can you trust what is real and what is misleading? How do you stay mindful when your mind wants to wander, explore, and create its own reality without permission?

The strategy I use to filter out the thoughts I don't need is a mental discipline that gets you to focus in on just the present moment. As most of your thoughts jump around and can be in the past one minute and the present the next, this form of mental conditioning—also known as **reframing your thinking portal**—works because it turns down the volume on noisy, intrusive thoughts.

Worry is conditioning your thoughts to fear. If you were raised by fearful parents, and spent most of your youth surrounded by fearful people, then being a worrier will seem the best course of action. This way, you build up your fears of the future and don't take any action for fear of failing.

Right now, make a list of three areas of your life you consistently worry about. Knowing what your triggers are plays a big part in this. Then, when you think about these areas, what thoughts enter your mind? Common themes are thoughts of scarcity, losing something valuable, failing fast, or being embarrassed if your master plan doesn't work out.

You might have fearful thoughts of money or relationships, worry about losing your job or getting ill. These are all legitimate worries. But worry leads to mental paralysis by default, and without taking positive action, you'll end up doing nothing. This ensures the worry habit sticks with its rotation and sets up a loop to capture your thoughts. You must unravel that loop and dismantle the worry habit.

You can empower your thoughts by feeding empowering messages to your mind. It works like the body. If you eat crap and junk food, you're going to feel like a physical garbage can. The mind is no different. Worrisome thoughts generate anxiety. You only get out of it what you feed into it.

Here is how you can eliminate the worry habit right now and gain control over the triggers that set you off.

Worry Thoughts are Fabrications

Worry is believing in false stories that have not come true. You worry about having no money, and yet, there is no evidence to suggest you will always be broke. Maybe you worry about your health and that you might get sick. Well, you will not be healthy forever, you know that. But you have your health today, don't you? Worrisome thoughts are grounded in future fear, like most things we stress about.

Worry is another form of fear. We create most of our fears.

They play out in our minds and take over all common sense. What are you worrying about right now? Is it something now or something supposed to happen later?

When you feed into the worry habit, you reinforce the false stories that will likely never happen.

From now on, feed your mind the good stuff it really wants. Try these affirmations instead:

- "I am not worried about tomorrow because today is perfect. The here and now is what I have."
- "I always worry about losing my job, but this has never happened to me. I am a good employee and the company I work for values its workers. Why would I think it could happen now?"

Break down your worrisome thoughts and expose these demons for what they are: False fabrications that rarely happen. Worry is a habit, and you can break any habit. But you can make your worrisome beliefs come true, too. If you believe that you will be broke, lose your health, or get divorced, then by carrying this worry around with you can manifest it to come true.

Remember: Thoughts have power and can draw toward you the bad as well as the good. If you think you're going to lose your job, you might show up at work acting like someone who doesn't deserve to be there.

Do you think your spouse is going to divorce you? This worry could cause you to become paranoid. Soon you start to track his or her whereabouts until they catch you planting a GPS unit underneath the car. So, while worrisome thinking is grounded in fantasy, you can manifest your worst nightmares to happen by holding onto these worrisome thoughts.

Negative Thinking: Hardwired for Fear

Positive thinking only works if you truly believe the message you're sending to your brain.

There are a few things I want to say about negative thinking. We tend to see negative thinking as something bad that you should be ashamed of. I'll admit that thinking positively and acting in a positive manner is much better than doing things in a negative way. But, it's a philosophy of mine that negative energy is just as important as positive energy.

How can that be?

You must walk through a mile of slimy mud sometimes before you can get to the green grass on the other end. In other words, being negative and experiencing the suffering that goes with it can be a great motivator for making the decision to change.

Negative thinking—or, "living a negative lifestyle", as I like to call it— is a sign that something is not right with your life. Believe it or not, some people seem to enjoy the attention they receive from negative thinking.

If you have an NMA (i.e., Negative Mental Attitude), and you are not happy with this, deciding to switch over to a positive frame of mind requires that you take intentional action to get your momentum moving.

Some of the world's greatest success stories have come from people who lived through hell and decided to change their lives. You can also look at the people who have everything going for them, and yet, they are unhappy, and it shows in their attitude.

I truly believe that living a positive lifestyle has very little to do with how much you own or how successful you are. It comes down to attitude in every aspect of your life. If all it took was money and popularity, then there wouldn't be any misery with people who seemingly have everything.

Thought and Circumstances: How to Attract What You Want

If you are unhappy with your present circumstances, whether it be your job, relationships, or current state of mind, there is only one way to change it: Think differently. I know this sounds like an obvious piece of advice, but there are reasons for this.

Do you know what happens when you think differently? Things on the outside begin to change. Your situation can only change if you do. Here is why.

Your outer world will always reflect the inner. Your success or failure is based on the success and failure going on inside. Succeed in programming your thoughts for having positive experiences and that is what will happen.

People have been known to alter the course of their lives with a shift in attitude. Can you imagine where you would be if you focused everything you had on thinking with a positive attitude? This isn't to say thinking alone will change you, but without it, we can't follow up with positive actions.

What exactly are positive actions? Some examples are: helping people, working toward goals that get you unstuck, streamlining your efforts to make life worth living for yourself and those around.

The circumstances of this life do not control you. While we can't always choose our circumstances, we can decide how to view them. It is just a matter of fact that bad things happen. Life doesn't go according to plan, and it isn't always fun—no matter who you are or how positive your thoughts may be. But you can train yourself in the best way to deal with it.